Stories

FROM MY Father

Lessons from Real Life

Lessons from Real Life

PAUL BOND, JR.

A Division of WINEPRESS PUBLISHING

ISBN 1-57921-659-5
Library of Congress Catalog Card Number: 2003104468

Dedication

This work is intended to glorify my Lord Jesus Christ. In Him is fullness of light and there is no darkness at all. All of the stories in each chapter are true. That is, they are stories handed down to me by oral tradition from people I've known or from members of my family. All the stories are recalled from my memory.

This small work is also dedicated to my daughters Mendy and Stephanie. I pray that they will always treasure their past and understand that their family was concerned about their walk with our Lord Jesus long before they were born.

I would also like to thank my wife, Gayle, who aided in the preparation of this manuscript. She is the love of my life. I know that she is truly a partner provided to me from God.

Table of Contents

CHAPTER 1

There Is Always a Father Who Loves

Years ago in the days of the Great Depression, young women growing up in the Ozark Mountains had few opportunities to find jobs off the farm or to ever move away from home. Usually when such an opportunity did arise, the girl would travel to a nearby city and work as a housekeeper or cook.

Ethel was related to me through marriage. It would take longer to explain how we are related than to tell you the rest of the story. I remember her as a slender woman with wide set eyes and a small chin. One day the impossible happened. Ethel had an opportunity to move off the farm at Clifty, Arkansas and move to Fayetteville and be the housekeeper for a prominent couple. She jumped at the chance.

The couple she worked for was fairly wealthy, well respected and well liked in the community. He was a tall, broad shouldered man, while the wife was short and slender. The couple had been childless for years but no one really understood why. Ethel worked hard for the couple cleaning their house and preparing their meals. For a while, everything appeared okay.

To this day it is not understood whether the sexual intercourse that took place between Ethel and her employer was consensual or not. All we do know is that Ethel became pregnant. Being an unwed mother is always a time of great stress, but especially so before World War II. Whom could she tell? How long before the obvious started to show? Would her employer harm her and her baby in order to protect his image? A thousand other questions went through her mind. However, Ethel did manage to pull herself together, and made her way back home where she told, of all people, her mother her situation.

Now at this point, a very strange thing happened. Ethel's mother decided that her daughter must marry so that the child will be legitimate and no shame would fall on the family name. Moreover, it must happen quickly. So on the same night Ethel returned home, Ethel's mother approached a young man in the community, Mr. Calico. Mr. Calico was a short, skinny man—almost frail. He listened to the explanation of the problem, considered the situation carefully and agreed to marry Ethel. So, the next day after she came home, Mr. Calico picked Ethel up at her mother's house and drove her to the nearest Justice of the Peace. There she stood before a JP and married a man she barely knew, Mr. Calico. After the ceremony, Mr. Calico dropped Ethel off at her mother's house and he went to his own home. As far as anyone knows, the marriage was never consummated.

Seven and half months later, a boy, Neal Calico, came into the world. There was no resemblance at all to his mother's husband. No matter. Mr. Calico loved his son.

As time passed, Ethel realized that she was grateful to Mr. Calico for all he had done to provide for her and her son, but she didn't love him. She wanted things Mr. Calico couldn't provide and she longed for the life of the city. So divorce came and she met and married a man she did love. Her new husband moved her back to Fayetteville and they started a new life together. Over time, Neal and his namesake father had less and less contact with each other. While Neal was fond of his new stepfather, the relationship between them was a little strained such that Neal didn't believe that he received much love or attention. Neal felt very lonely and isolated most of the time.

Years went by. Neal grew up to be a tall broad shouldered young man (very unlike his namesake father) and after high school, joined the Air Force. While stationed in Wichita, KS, Neal received a letter from a girl back home that he had envisioned would one day be his bride. The letter stated that she would marry someone else and that she hoped he would understand. Despondent over all the broken relationships in his life and convinced that in this world he would never know love, Neal drove himself off base, pulled a large caliber pistol out of the glove box of his car, put it to his head and committed suicide.

At the funeral, there was another strange sight. On the front row, but not sitting with the family, was a small frail man. The man who loved Neal like a son. The man who was willing to give Neal his last name, Mr. Calico. Possibly the only person whom, given enough time, may have been able to prevent this awful scene. He had come to say goodbye to his only son, a son he gave his name to, but one he was unable to have much of a relationship with.

Neal Calico's story is true. I know because every spring I walk by his grave and give my regards to the cousin I never knew. But in Neal's story, I see four wonderful truths that we all should understand: We are all born into sin, we all have a heavenly Father who loves us a great deal, we all have need to turn from darkness to light, and finally, we all need families that understand our worst failures.

According to William J. Bennett's book, *The Index of Leading Cultural Indicators,*[1] in 1960 only five percent of all births were to unwed mothers. No wonder in the past there was such a stigma attached to being born without a father. From the same source, we find that in 1997, one out of three children born in the U.S. were born unto unwed mothers. The stigma may be gone, but the root cause is still the same. We are all born into sin. I am not saying all sex is sinful. I am not saying that because of sin we all exist. What I am trying to point out is that we are all born with a predisposition to rebel against a Father we may not know very well. We are separated from a Father who loves us a great deal; circumstances have dictated (so it seems) that we go our own way. Listen to the words from the gospel of John:

John 3:19–21 [19]This, then, is the judgment: the light has come into the world, and people loved darkness rather than the light because their deeds were evil. [20]For everyone who practices wicked things hates the light and avoids it [and does not come into the light], so that his deeds may not be exposed. [21]But anyone who lives by the truth comes to the light, so that his works may be shown to be accomplished by God. *HCSB*[2]

God is light. This is a radical thought. Light from the sun embodies the full spectrum of color visible to the human eye (if I remember my high school physics). It is pure and without contamination. Light is warm. The whole of our ecosystem here on earth is powered by the warmth from our sun. Thus, if God is light, He must be pure and uncontaminated, warm and welcoming, full of life, able to give life and full of every color imaginable.

Darkness is cold, lifeless and contains a million shades of gray and black. No other colors need apply. Here then is the strange truth: people love darkness more than light. When given a choice, people choose to take care of themselves, to do what is right in their own eyes, to tackle the problems in their life with the resources available within their own minds, to get what they want because they want it. All of this is darkness. People love darkness rather than light.

In Neal's story, this darkness is illustrated by two episodes: An employer who has sexual relations with an employee half his age and Ethel's continuing desire to have more of the material things of this world.

If in light there is life, then the eventual outcome of darkness is death. Nocturnal predators live by consuming those animals that thrive in the light. Over time, however, even the nocturnal predator meets the same end as did their prey—they die. Is it not strange then, that we humans feel ourselves to be so superior that we do not need a loving Father? The outcome of our self-pride is evident from the very beginning in that darkness always leads to death. Why choose darkness and death? Why not come to know the Father who has loved you more dearly than any human has the capacity to love?

Like Mr. Calico, we all have a heavenly Father who loves us dearly. We may not know Him, we may not hear His voice or see His face, yet He is always there. Things have happened to separate us from our Father, but He shows us His love through time and space. Listen to the words of the apostle Paul:

> Romans 5:8 [8]But God proves His own love for us in that while we were still sinners Christ died for us! *HCSB*[2]

God loves you with an indescribable love. He wants you to turn from the ways that will kill you. But he won't force himself on you. You must be willing to go to Him. And when we accept Him into our lives, like Mr. Calico, He gives us His name. Listen again to words from the apostle John:

> 1 John 3:1 [1]See how very much our heavenly Father loves us, for he allows us to be called his children, *and we really are!* But the people who belong to this world don't

know God, so they don't understand that we are his children. *NLT*[3] (emphasis added)

These verses clearly tell of the love God has for us. As Henry Blackaby says, "Your love for me was settled on the cross. That has never changed and will never change for me."[5] The coming of Christ is God's ultimate expression of His love for mankind. I've often wondered how many times Mr. Calico thought of the boy he had given his name to all through those years of separation. Likewise, I wonder how many times those who are His children, as well as those who still choose to dwell in the darkness, are on the mind of God. If He cared enough to send all he had, all He ever would have to show His love for me, I must be on His mind often. So are you.

But it goes beyond that. Not only has He shown His love for us, like Mr. Calico, He is willing to give us His name. He is willing to adopt us into His family. When a Roman citizen adopted a child, that child obtained the same privileges and rights as the firstborn. The firstborn child a Roman could disown. An adopted child was his forever.

Being an adopted child of God results in the child having a measure of power and authority as he walks through this world. Listen to the words of Jesus found in the Gospel of Matthew:

Matthew 18:18–20 [18]I assure you: Whatever you bind on earth will have been bound in heaven, and what ever you loose on earth will have been loosed in heaven. [19] Again, I assure you: If two of you on earth agree about any matter that you pray for, it will be done for you by

My Father in heaven. [20] For where two or three are gathered together in My name, I am there among them. *HCSB*[2]

Our prayers are answered. Our difficulties are made easier to overcome. Our fellowship with each other is made complete by his promised presence. All of this because He chooses to let us use His name. Mr. Calico gave Neal his name. All Mr. Calico had in this world (however small or great that might have been) could have been Neal's if Neal had chosen to have a relationship with Mr. Calico. Instead, Neal chose suicide. But like Neal, too many times, people enter eternity without the knowledge of a Father who desperately loves them and would remove any barrier to have a relationship with them if only they appeared interested. I can not prove this with Scripture, but it is my opinion that God, like Mr. Calico, attends every funeral given, knows of every homeless, nameless person who dies alone on a sidewalk, and is present in every womb where an unborn child is literally ripped apart and aborted. Like Mr. Calico, He weeps for what might have been. Conversely, the psalmist tells us:

Psalm 116:15 [15]Precious in the sight of the LORD is the death of his saints. *NIV*[4]

We all have a need to turn from darkness to light. Everyone born has a bit of darkness in his or her heart. Since we know that God is light, the solution to our darkness is evident. With God in our heart, the darkness is removed. It is impossible for darkness to dwell in the presence of light. Remember those words from the Gospel of John?

John 3:21a ²¹But anyone who lives by the truth comes to the light. *HCSB*²

Therefore, it is possible to change our understanding and knowledge of God. While in darkness, we may question if there is a God. Or if God is really a Father of love, why does so much suffering exist in the world? After we come to the light, we understand the nature of God much differently. How much suffering did Neal endure his whole life? Remember I told you of his loneliness, his feelings of being unloved and his heartbreak over broken relationships. Through all of Neal's sufferings, did Mr. Calico fail to love his son? NO. The problem was Mr. Calico and Neal were not in right relationship with each other. The same is true with us and God. If we refuse to know Him, if we refuse to give Him our lives, if we refuse to be in right relationship to Him, we have no grounds to complain about our sufferings or the sufferings of others. We have brought suffering upon ourselves because we have refused God's love.

Again, I offer an opinion: No one really wants to dwell in darkness their whole life. Even the most hardened of rebels hope that somewhere a friend, a parent or a grandparent is praying to God for their soul. Only the truly deceived think they want to dwell in darkness forever and to keep their lives in the *status quo*. Have you ever been on a tour of a cave? What happens when they get you to the bottom of the cave? They always do this. It never fails. They turn off the lights so you can experience total darkness. Do you remember how that felt? How your eyes almost were in pain because they longed to see light. In those moments, I have literally put my hand in front of my face.

I knew it was there because I could feel my hand at the end of my nose. Yet I could not see my hand. But my eyes longed to see. Remember what happens next? Your tour guide lights a match. Or they turn on a flashlight. Your eyes are immediately drawn to that light and you cannot focus on anything other than that small light. The nerve endings in our eyes fire or go off at the stimulus of light, they rest during sleep but total darkness seems to cause harm. So it is with God. In total darkness, we long for some point of light somewhere. Our spirits are only stimulated by the presence of God (spiritual light), and when there is none, we are nearly in pain. But when God appears, the spirit can only concentrate on Him. Have you ever passed from darkness to light? If you want to know the Father's love, if you want to be assured you have passed from darkness to light, there are helps in the appendix of this book. This I do know: in the words of the old gospel song, "Where there's a flicker of sunlight on the far side of midnight, stands Jesus beyond a shadow of a doubt."

We all need families that understand our worst failures. We need families that accept us and love us after we fail. We need families to support us when we are the victim. When Ethel found herself in trouble, her response was to leave a situation where she might be harmed further and go back home. Back home, she confided in her mother about all her difficulties and found a solution. A perfect solution? No. But a solution she was able to live with. How many children today would be able to find a solace back home?

First, let's touch upon the fact that it is harder to define what "family" or "a home" means. Again I quote from William J. Bennett's *The Index of Leading Cultural Indicators*[1] (ILCI) where he says one in three children live in a single parent home. Of the remainder, chances are the child is living as a stepchild. The vast minority of kids grow up in a home where Dad has always loved Mom, they have been married since dirt was new and will remain married long after the kids move out. This being the situation, what type of spiritual help will a child find at home?

The *ILCI* tells us that for the last forty years, around sixty percent of Americans possess church membership. A Gallop poll reported that ninety-six percent of Americans believed in a god or "universal spirit," but about half attend church less than once per month or never. Thus, we give God a good deal of lip service, and very little of our time. This is evident by the increases in the numbers of people who cohabitate unmarried, the increases in unwed mothers and the fact you need a dictionary to define family. We are now a society where everything is relative; there are no absolutes. The Bible is full of absolutes, but we don't heed them. We are intellectual, we are progressive and we are smarter than God. We are also overrun with darkness. The prophet Isaiah wrote:

> Isaiah 29:13–15 [13]The Lord says: "These people come near to me with their mouth and honor me with their lips, but their hearts are far from me. Their worship of me is made up only of rules taught by men. [14]Therefore once more I will astound these people with wonder upon

wonder; the wisdom of the wise will perish, the intelligence of the intelligent will vanish." [15]Woe to those who go to great depths to hide their plans from the LORD, who do their work in DARKNESS and think, "Who sees us? Who will know?" *NIV*[4] (emphasis added)

When we come from darkness into light, we understand a great truth. What is done in our lives could not happen under our own strength, but is a demonstration of the power of God. Remember the Gospel of John:

John 3:21 [21]But anyone who lives by the truth comes to the light, so that his works may be shown to be accomplished by God. *HCSB*[2]

With that in mind, we understand that the spiritual help we give our children is not a reflection of how great we are as parents, but rather a manifestation of the workings of God. On our own, children are an enigma and their problems impossible to solve. With God, nothing comes our way that He can't handle, no matter how outrageous or egregious.

All too often has someone entered eternity, like my cousin Neal, without knowing that they have a spiritual Father who is waiting in the shadows to love them. What we should come to understand is that we have a heavenly, spiritual Father who loves us more than we will ever realize. Like Mr. Calico, He yearns to fellowship with us and to give us His name. The god of materialism may not make a change in the way people think or behave or even remove their darkness. But the God I know, like Mr. Calico, has the potential to radically change individuals and families by bringing them into His light.

CHAPTER 2

A Father of Grace

I remember that the summer of 1967 was dry and hot. The city had just installed a water line in our neighborhood. However, Mom and Dad didn't think that they wanted to pay the city of Fayetteville money every month for their chlorinated, guaranteed germ free, ill-tasting water when we had water from a well that tasted sweet and was free of cost. Since it had been some time since rain had fallen, the water table in the well was low. Dad told me not to use too much water because there wasn't much of it. When I bathed, when I brushed my teeth, when I did anything with water, remember not to use too much, because the well was just about dry. Thus, I knew and understood the rule—don't use too much water.

For my sixth birthday in December of 1966, I received two gifts. One was a Lionel 027 gauge electric toy train. I still have it; you can come out to the house to watch it run if you wish. The second was a Montgomery Ward bicycle. It was red with a white "banana" seat and high handlebars.

This particular day, I had been riding my bike a long while and, because it was dry, my bike became coated with dust. It needed a wash, don't you think?

So, I turned on the water and washed off my bike. I watered the few flowers that were still alive. I washed off (that is, sprayed water on) the windows of our house. I watered a lot of stuff. I ran water, and ran water and ran water. I noticed that the water suddenly turned from clear to a muddy brown. Not being much of a plumber at age six, it seemed to me that the obvious solution to this situation was to let the water run more. Surely clear water would come out of the hose if only this muddy stuff would go away. But the more the water ran, the more brown the color and the more muddy it became. Finally, with a spluttering sound and a sort of wheeze, the water stopped coming out of the hose all together.

Suddenly, I realized what I had done and fear, like a bolt of lightening, overwhelmed my being because I realized I had broken the rule. I had used too much water and now the well was dry. It was going to be hard to hide this one. Not only had I used too much water, but it was all spent for such frivolous pursuits. I was fearful, worried and deeply disappointed in myself. At that point, I looked up, and there stood my dad looking at me. I knew the rule, and I broke it. I was caught with the hose in my hand looking and being extremely guilty. What would become of me and how would my family have water? Answers to these questions just didn't seem to matter when your dad is staring you down.

Just as I was at that point in time, all of mankind stands before God guilty of breaking God's rules. Whether we've ever been taught the rules or not, we know them almost intuitively . . . don't hurt your neighbor, don't steal from your neighbor, don't lie, respect God. However, just in case some have never heard, let's briefly review a few verses from the book of Exodus:

> Exodus 20:1–4a, 7–8a, 12–17a: [1]And God spoke all these words: [2]"I am the LORD your God who brought you out of Egypt, out of the land of slavery. [3]You shall have no other gods before me. [4]You shall not make for yourself an idol . . . [7]You shall not misuse the name of the LORD your God, for the LORD will not hold anyone guiltless who misuses his name. [8]Remember the Sabbath day by keeping it holy . . . [12]Honor [highly prize, care for, show respect for and obey] your father and your mother, so that you may live long in the land the LORD your God is giving you. [13]You shall not murder. [14]You shall not commit adultery. [15]You shall not steal. [16]You shall not give false testimony against your neighbor. [17]You shall not covet . . . NIV[4]

Here then are the standards of conduct as set by the living God. Since God is light, there are no ambiguities in the rules: no fog, no shades of gray. Just eight "You shall nots" and two "You shalls." The first four deal with our behavior towards Him. The next five deal with our behavior toward our fellow man. Curiously, the last deals with the condition of the human heart that initiates all the other behaviors. Remember from the last chapter that:

John 3:20 [20]For everyone who practices wicked things hates the light and avoids it [and does not come into the light], so that his deeds may not be exposed. *HCSB*[2]

The term wicked does not describe the "Wicked Witch of the West" from the *Wizard of Oz*, but rather describes a stick or a piece of lumber that is crooked. Being wicked means not being straight. To covet is a wicked practice. We desire what we cannot, at the moment, have. Every advertising agency on Madison Avenue would have to lock its doors tomorrow if we all stopped coveting. The ads just wouldn't work anymore. I believe what God is trying to teach us here is that most outward behaviors toward Him or our fellow men is a direct result of what is in our heart. If darkness overwhelms our thoughts and mind, then we do and say things that ultimately harm those around us. Thus, we avoid God because His light exposes our darkness; His standards expose our deficiencies.

Unfortunately, many people believe, and some religions teach, that if you just don't break the rules and keep the standards of God, you are guaranteed the possession of light (what Baptists refer to as salvation). Their motivation is that through self-discipline and obedience to rules, they will be made perfect. This is similar to the New Age idea that inside each of us is divinity. If we work hard enough on ourselves, eventually the divine will come out. This is totally false and a lie of the Deceiver. What we fail to perceive is that when Jesus Christ came into the world, He did not applaud the above standards, but rather He changed them by elevating them. He made them more difficult to keep. In fact, they are so difficult to keep as to be impossible. Look at the Gospel of Matthew:

> Matthew 5:21–22 [21]You have heard that it was said to our ancestors, '**You shall not murder**,' and whoever murders [a deliberate, premeditated act] will be subject to judgment. [22]But I tell you, everyone who is angry with his brother [some texts add "without a cause"] will be subject to judgment. And whoever says to his brother, 'Fool!' will be subject to the council. But whoever says, 'You Moron!' will be subject to [the fires of *gehenna*] hellfire. *HCSB*[2] (Note: the Gehenna valley outside of Jerusalem was once a place of child sacrifice. In the time of Jesus, it served as the garbage dump of Jerusalem and most often served as His illustration of what hell was like, as fires continually burned there.)

Therefore the standard of perfection that Jesus gave us is not outward behavior, but the attitude of our hearts and the words that leave our lips. If darkness controls the majority of our heart, our actions are motivated by that darkness and not light. Not many people traveling through a city on a freeway haven't expressed their belief that other persons driving in other vehicles possess less than optimum intelligence (did I say that nicely enough?). That is, all of us have called someone else a moron at least once in our lives. We all have had attitudes and thoughts towards God, someone else or even ourselves that were filled with darkness. (For example: She's fat. He's stupid. God surely doesn't love someone like me. All these thoughts are based in darkness.) We know the rules, and we've broken the rules. No one is perfect. Romans 3:23 says:

25

Romans 3:23 [23]For all have sinned and fall short of the glory of God. *HCSB* [2]

"For all have messed up and have failed to live up to God's standards," Paul Bond, Jr.'s paraphrased version.

Notice three other things. First, my messing up and running the well dry affected more people than just me. Because the well was now dry, my whole family did not have drinking water. No water for washing of clothes or bathing. We, as a family, were in trouble. Failing to live up to God's standards will always affect the people around you. Society as a whole suffers because we as individuals mess up. More people will be affected by your messing up than you can ever imagine.

Secondly, I also want to point out that my transgression lasted much longer than I thought it would. That day as a six-year-old boy, I assumed that the water would return to the well after the next rain. However, just a few years ago, in the late 1990's, my mother had the well house torn down and the well filled. Guess what? Thirty-two years later, the well was still dry. When I mess up, I do it very skillfully. When we fail to keep God's standards, the consequences may last much longer than we will ever know.

Third, my messing up was impossible to hide. My dad didn't have to catch me with a spluttering water hose in my hand to find out the well was dry. All he had to do was turn on the faucet at the nearest sink. All of us think our sin is hidden. Truth is, God sees it all the time. And you know what? In spite of that sin, that messing up of our lives, He loves us anyway. See the previous chapter for details.

The breaking of rules and messing up always comes at a price. In Old Testament times, disobedience came at a very high price. Look closely at the words of Moses found in the book of Leviticus (I warn you, the following is not for the faint of heart):

> Leviticus 4:27–31 [27]If a member of the community sins unintentionally and does what is forbidden in any of the LORD's commands, he is guilty. [28]When he is made aware of the sin he committed, he must bring as his offering for the sin he committed a female goat without defect. [29]He is to lay his hand on the head of the sin offering and slaughter it at the place of the burnt offering. [30]Then the priest is to take some of the blood with his finger and put it on the horns of the altar of burnt offering and pour out the rest of the blood at the base of the altar. [31]He shall remove all the fat, just as the fat is removed from the fellowship offering, and the priest shall burn it on the altar as an aroma pleasing to the LORD. In this way the priest will make atonement for him, and he will be forgiven. NIV[4]

Thus, the price of disobedience was the life of another living thing. Blood was the price of messing up and the cost of atonement (making things right again). The shedding of blood was not something taken lightly. The guilty party had to place his hand on the head of the animal as a sign of the transference of guilt from himself to the animal, then the animal was killed. This begs the question, if the transference had not taken place, who should die? Certainly not the animal. The animal had not disobeyed.

Why does the thought of the shedding of innocent sacrificial blood seem so repugnant to us in modern times? Answer: because we don't have to perform sacrifices anymore. We don't lay hands on an innocent animal and pray for a transference of guilt from me to it. Why? Because through the sacrifice of one truly perfect being called the Lamb of God and the Light we no longer kill animals because of our messing up. Jesus took care of it once for all. He died once for all mankind. Listen to the words of the writer of the book of Hebrews:

> Hebrews 10:1, 4, 10b, 14 [1]The law is only a shadow of the good things that are coming—not the realities themselves. For this reason it can never, by the same sacrifices repeated endlessly year after year, make perfect those who draw near to worship ... [4]because it is impossible for the blood of bulls and goats to take away sins ... [10b]we have been made holy through the sacrifice of the body of Jesus Christ once for all ... [14]because by one sacrifice he has made perfect forever those who are being made holy. *NIV*[4]

Much to the dismay of animal rights activists, orthodox Jews hope to one day have a new temple standing upon the Temple Mount in Jerusalem and to reinstate animal sacrifice.

As my dad stood there looking at me and I was holding that garden hose in my hand with nothing coming out, he had a decision to make. Dad could hear the pump in the pump house running, yet nothing was coming from the hose. Thus, Dad had complete understanding of what was going on, and he had to choose from two alternatives. First, he could give me what I deserved and punish me, not pay the price for hooking on to the new water line (with the city's chlorinated, guaranteed germ free, ill-tasting water), let the family thirst to death and from then on, he and I would be enemies. Or he could choose grace, pay the price for a tap on the new water line and forgive me. After a long period of silence that seemed like centuries . . . Dad chose grace.

Until the end of this world, God always chooses grace. That one time, my earthly father chose grace. Our heavenly Father always chooses grace. Because God recognized that animal sacrifices are not enough to build a relationship with mankind, He knew a better way had to be found. This better way would involve man being deeply intimate with Him, the living God. So, long ago, God spoke to the prophet Jeremiah and said:

> Jeremiah 31:31–34 [31]"The time is coming," declares the LORD, "when I will make a new covenant [a contract or agreement] with the house of Israel and with the house of Judah. [32]It will not be like the covenant I made with their forefathers when I took them by the hand to lead them out of Egypt, because they broke my covenant, though I was a husband to them," declares the LORD. [33]"This is the covenant I will make with the house of Israel after that time," declares the LORD. "I will put my law in their minds and write it on their hearts. I will be their God, and they will be my people. [34]No longer will

a man teach his neighbor, or a man his brother, saying 'Know the Lord,' because they will all KNOW me, from the least of them to the greatest," declares the LORD. "For I will FORGIVE their WICKEDNESS and will remember their sins no more." *NIV*[4] (emphasis added)

From this statement of God to Jeremiah, we find that God recognized that the keeping of rules was inadequate for us to come to fully understand Him. He is not a God of rules. He is full of grace. He chose to make Himself known to everyone willing to listen to Him. He chose to forgive. He promises not to remember our messing up anymore. Why? If you remember nothing else about this chapter or about this entire book, I hope you remember these next words:

Isaiah 43:25 I, even I, am he who blots our your transgressions, for MY OWN SAKE, and remembers your sins no more. *NIV*[4] (emphasis added)

and the words of the apostle John:

1 John 2:12 I write to you, dear children, because your sins have been forgiven on account of his name NIV[4] or, your sins are forgiven you for His name's sake. NKJV[6]

The amazing thing about God is that He longs and desires to have fellowship, to have a relationship with you and me. Therefore, He was willing to pay any price imaginable to get to know you. In the previous chapter, Mr. Calico was willing to take in a young woman in trouble and to provide for her so that he might have an heir. Mr. Calico was willing to pay a price. Dad went down to city hall and paid the fee for a tap on the new water line for the city of Fayetteville's chlorinated, guaranteed germ-free, ill-tasting water. He paid the price so his family would not thirst and he chose not to punish his one and only son. The verses above tell us that God willingly removed every barrier in heaven and on earth to pay the price for you to know Him, even though the price was His one and only son, Jesus Christ. He did this for HIS OWN SAKE. It is the nature of God to have fellowship with people, to have fellowship with you, to talk with you and you to Him. Unfortunately, most of us just stand around with the garden hose in our hand looking and feeling guilty because of the sin in our lives instead of enjoying God's grace. God always chooses grace. What have you chosen?

The words of the apostle Paul sum up this chapter very well:

> Romans 8:1–4 [1]Therefore, there is now no condemnation for those who are in Christ Jesus, [2]because through Christ Jesus the law of the Spirit of life set me free from the law of sin and death. [3]For what the law was powerless to do in that it was weakened by the sinful nature, God did by sending his own Son in the likeness of sinful man to be a sin offering. And so he condemned sin in sinful man, in order that the righteous requirements of the law might be fully met in us, who do not live according to the sinful nature but according to the Spirit. *NIV*[4]

Since God is light, His remedy for my mistakes and messing up is very clear. He sent everything He had, everything He ever hoped to have, in order to pay the price for my messing up. He chose grace and forgave me just as my earthly father forgave me for running the well dry. He chooses grace for your life as well and is willing to forgive you if you are willing to accept it. Saying to yourself that you are a decent person and you will be okay when facing God is relying on the darkness of obeying rules. God's light is this: the rules show us we can't live up to His standards. Knowing this, He is willing to pay our debt for rule breaking, and is willing to forgive us. If you wish to make certain you have passed from darkness to light, see the end of the book for help.

CHAPTER 3

Shades of Gray and a Father of Mercy

H
e was the youngest of the four children born to Sid and Anna Belle. He was taller than his brothers and broader across the shoulders. He had a happy-go-lucky attitude about most things. Very seldom would you see him without a mischievous grin on his face and a twinkle in his eye. Roy was well liked and perhaps a little spoiled by his parents. Due to his parents' inability to control Roy's behavior (more than once he locked his mother in a closet), it was decided he should join the army and learn some self discipline. Unfortunately for Roy, his parents made this decision in 1942.

After Boot Camp, Roy had a short leave back home before shipping off to serve in the European theater in World War II. He was assigned to the "Golden Acorn" Division, the stalwart 87th, which fought with General Patton's 3rd army. In December of 1944, the group found themselves caught up in the Battle of the Bulge. Things became tense back home until a letter that Roy wrote arrived to say he survived the onslaught. Contact with Roy was infrequent, but at least Sid and Anna Belle knew their son was alive. Nightly, Anna Belle would listen to the news on the radio to learn of the latest happenings from the front. Nightly she prayed for the safety of her youngest son. Then the telegram came.

"Your son has been wounded in battle. Stop. Further details to follow."

Days turned into weeks and no word about the whereabouts or fate of Roy had been forth coming. The silence seemed to last for an eternity. Sick and depressed over sending their boy into battle, Sid and Anna Belle fought off depression. Finally, my Aunt Dorothy picked up a telephone and called a congressman. What happened? A miracle. It was learned that Roy was in a hospital in France. Shell-shocked from his ordeal, he was alive, but his progress had been slow.

Later, it was learned that, after the 87th had crossed the Rhine River, Roy had been on patrol with three other men. The leader of this small group of men stepped on a land mine. Roy was the only one of the four to survive. After a long rehabilitation period, Roy was reassigned to a non-combat role. For his sacrifice, Roy was awarded the Purple Heart.

After the war, Roy married and started a family. Moving to the community of Baldwin, Arkansas, just east of Fayetteville, he joined his father and oldest brother in the family business of water well drilling. He was well liked by his neighbors and was known for his sense of humor as well as sense of fair play. But, like all of us at one point in our lives, Roy had one overriding problem: he was without Christ. He did not have a relationship with our heavenly Father.

That too changed one day when his brother urged him to come to a church and hear the word of God. What happened? A miracle. He went. He heard. He believed. He walked an aisle. He accepted Christ and was baptized a few days later. Roy passed from darkness to light.

However, it seemed no one else in his family followed his lead. This was especially true of his wife who now found living with Roy 'boring', so she started 'dating' other men. Infidelity, coupled with anger, attacked their relationship and eventually there was a divorce. Roy always carried bitterness in his heart about this chapter in his life and it was a bitterness that he never recovered from. At this low point, however, Roy had a choice to make in his life. He could choose to keep following Christ and pray that one day his marriage would be made whole or he could choose to act the way the world told him to act. He made a lousy decision. He chose drink over God, the old life over the new. Bad went to worse.

However, God always appeared to be reaching out to Roy. In the book of Proverbs we read:

Proverbs 3:12 [12]For whom the Lord loves He corrects,
Just as a father the son *in whom* he delights. *NKJV*[6]

In the late 1960's, Roy tried on his own to straighten up and he remarried. But alcoholism still had a big hold on his life, and thus, the marriage did not last long. Finally, after years of drinking, he became very ill. He would have headaches that would last for days on end. The doctors discovered an aneurysm in his brain. They explained that if they repaired the blood vessel surgically, he would almost have a 50-50 shot at living. Not removing the aneurysm meant certain death. Brain surgery was risky so there was also a good chance Roy wouldn't survive the operation. Roy consented to the surgery. He was taken to the Veterans Administration Hospital in Little Rock where they shaved his head, cut open his skull and attempted to repair the damaged blood vessel. What happened? A miracle. Roy survived the surgery, his aneurysm was gone, and he was able to live again. However, before the surgery, Roy suffered a stroke which did damage some of his motor skills such that he limped and his right arm was gnarled.

Unfortunately, the lessons God was trying to teach Roy (that life is precious and we shouldn't waste life being bitter and that God longed for a renewed relationship with Roy) didn't sink in. Roy spent too much time listening to the wrong advice. Old habits die hard, and cheap whiskey and wine soon regained their foothold in his life. After two divorces, medical bills and a daily tab at the liquor store, Roy lost almost everything he owned. Now drinking again, he had no place to live but the camper on the back of his pickup truck (the truck was parked at the residence of his oldest brother), nothing to wear but blue jeans, a western shirt, a floppy old cowboy hat and some red cowboy boots. He made daily trips to the liquor store, and you could see him limping from the store to his truck every day with a brown paper bag under his arm while wearing his red boots, floppy cowboy hat and all.

In 1977, my high school (Fayetteville High) had open campus for lunch. Eleven thirty rolled around and it seemed as if 10,000 cars roared out of the parking lot and headed for the nearest eatery. Pizza. Burgers. Now and then a salad. The favorite place my friends and I frequented was a burger joint called *Mr. Quick*. One particular day, we sat in a booth by the window. As we ate, walking down the road across from the café, was a familiar figure with red boots, a floppy hat and brown bag under his arm. My friend Mitchell said, "Look at that old coot. Looks like he's going to tie one on." I have done very few things in my life that were honorable, but on that day I finally did something right. I replied, "Mitchell, that's not just an old coot, as you call him, that's my Uncle Roy."

Roy Lee Bond died in December of 1980, a week to the day after my maternal grandmother passed away. More unnerving than going to two funerals within a week is the lack of confidence I have in Roy's salvation experience. God is light. Men love darkness more than light. Even when a person receives the light of Christ, if he or she chooses to let that light diminish or go dark, we no longer see light but a thousand shades of gray. The grayness of shadows always brings with it uncertainty, confusion and apprehension. God is also a Father of mercy who understands the heart. He knows who truly possesses light and who doesn't. It is much better to live a life full of His merciful light than to dwell constantly in shadows. This begs the question: is my life, is your life, full of light or just a thousand shades of gray?

> Matthew 10:32–33 [32] Therefore, whoever confesses Me before men, him I will also confess before my Father who is in heaven. [33] But whoever denies Me before men, him I will also deny before My father who is in heaven. *NKJV*[6]

More precious to us than our earthly relatives is our standing and relationship with the living God. If we can stand up for our earthly relatives, how much more should we be willing to stand up and live a life which glorifies our heavenly Father? Since He is light, if we claim to have a relationship with Him, then some of His light should shine through our darkness. If His light is shining in our lives, we then are confessing Him before all who look our way. Confessing Christ is much more that walking an aisle and accepting Christ publicly. It is daily living a life of light. Nothing is more confusing to those who are standing in darkness than to see the people of the light not being light at all, but gray. All too often, we are like Roy, in that there are so many shades of gray in our lives that it is hard to find the Light. Sometimes, I think the Father looks out the window of heaven and sees me with the red cowboy boots of pride on my feet, the floppy cowboy hat of selfishness on my head, with a brown bag full of my own foolish plans under my arm as I stagger through life under my own power. An angel asks, "Who is that?" and God replies, "Oh, that's just Paul. He's one of ours you know."

God has made a way for us who have come to the light to stay in His light. Because He is light, it is a simple two-step process. First of all, we must recognize that when we accepted Jesus Christ into our lives, when we accepted His atonement, a great thing happened. He forgave us of all our sin, our messing up. The sins of yesterday are gone and forgotten. The sin of today is gone and forgotten. The sin of tomorrow is like it never will happen. God's atonement was so complete there is not a way in your life where you mess up that Jesus wasn't aware of on the cross and that He did not die for. The price for our rule breaking is paid in full! Secondly, God recognized that His people of light can get dirty walking through this world. Just like a light bulb in a livestock barn can become covered with dust and dirt, a Christian can become covered with the dirt of this world. The remedy for this is called confession. Consider this principle in Scripture:

> Exodus 12:14–15 [14] This is the day you are to commemorate; for the generations to come you shall celebrate it as a festival to the Lord—a lasting ordinance. [15] For seven days you are to eat bread made without yeast. On the first day remove the yeast from your houses, for whoever eats anything with yeast in it from the first day through the seventh must be cut off from Israel. NIV[4]

Before the Hebrews could see God do a great work on their behalf and before they could prepare to see the hand of the Lord by celebrating the first Passover and leaving Egypt, what did they have to do? Remove the yeast from their homes. To this day, before the Passover celebration starts, a Jewish family goes throughout their whole house and removes anything that contains yeast, mildew or fungus. Anything and everything. Their homes must be completely clean and absent of yeast, mold and mildew before the preparation of the meal can start. We Gentiles call this spring cleaning. How does this custom affect a Christian?

> 1 Corinthians 5:6b–8 [6B] Don't you know that a little yeast permeates the whole batch of dough? [7] Clean out the old yeast so that you may be a new batch, since you are unleavened. For Christ our Passover has been sacrificed. [8] Therefore, let us observe the feast, not with old yeast, or with the yeast of malice and evil, but with the unleavened bread of sincerity and truth. HCSB [2]

Here the apostle Paul states in verse eight that the true yeast God is concerned with is a spiritual yeast, a mold called sin. Just as the Jews clean their physical homes of yeast once per year, we need to periodically clean our hearts of the stains this world throws at us. This spring cleaning of the heart and life is called confession. If we don't throw out the yeast and mold of sin periodically, we stay dirty. If you don't dust off a light bulb, it stays dirty. And the problem with a little sin in our life, according to verse six is what? It affects the whole lump of dough. That is, your sin not only affects you, it affects your family, your church and your whole community. Remember the last chapter and how I ran the well dry? The effects of yeast are similar.

My mother was famous in our hometown for her homemade rolls. Bread made with yeast. For a time, she was employed by a local church as hostess where she would prepare a meal for as many as 250 people. I have personally stood in the kitchen of that church and helped my mother prepare the dough for those rolls. She would add the ingredients together in a bowl. Flour, water, sugar, oil, eggs and salt. Finally, she would add the yeast, stir all the ingredients together and then leave the bowl in a warm, shadowy place. After a while, the yeast would have performed its job and the little lump of dough would have grown out of the bowl to the point it nearly would stretch down and touch the counter top. At this point, Mom would cut the dough in tiny pieces, dip each piece in butter, place the piece in a pan and place the pan in the oven. Sometimes thirty dozen rolls would appear out of one lump of dough. Why? Because a little bit of yeast affected the whole lump of dough. Our messing up always starts out small. We only break one little rule. But before all is said and done, things have turned into a big mess. It may seem small at first, but notice what the Gospel of Luke has to say:

> Luke 12:1b–3 [1b]Be on your guard against the yeast of the Pharisees, which is hypocrisy. [2]There is nothing covered that won't be uncovered; nothing hidden that won't be made known. [3]Therefore whatever you have said in the dark will be heard in the light, and what you have whispered in an ear in private rooms will be proclaimed on the housetops. HCSB [2]

Verse one tells us not to be filled with hypocrisy. The original word in the Greek refers to an actor or someone who pretends to be something he is not. People of the light who walk in shades of gray are usually play actors. They are telling others they are okay when, in fact, trouble has camped deep inside their life. My point is that all of us are hypocrites of one stripe or another. We all act out roles now and then. We tell our mother-in-law we love her, then spend the next 364 days putting her down verbally. We attend a Republican event and then vote Democratic. We wear an Atlanta Braves jersey, but we really are a Yankees fan. The worst excuse I've ever heard about why someone would not become a Christian, to step from darkness to light, is that "They are all just a bunch of hypocrites." Yes, the church is full of hypocrites. But so is Wal-Mart, K-Mart, Target, our place of business, the grocery store and the post office. We all have times in our lives when we act. But I digress. The question should be, "Why do we act?"

Look closely at verses two and three of the passage above because they reveal the answer. Why don't we see more people confess their sin and stop playacting? They think their sin is covered up. They think no one sees what's wrong, where they've messed up. They forget that God sees and knows more about it than they do. "No one knows but me," they tell themselves. "It is such a little thing, really." Just remember, what's covered will be revealed, there's nothing hidden that won't be made known. We all want the light of God in our lives, but some of us just don't want that light to shine too brightly, because it would reveal some stuff we have hidden in that dark corner of our heart. We want God in our lives, just so long as He is a 40 watt bulb. You know, nothing too intrusive. "I have MY plans, you know. So, I don't want a god that is a spot light. I have some stuff in the corner of my heart, over in the dark, that I would just as soon no one knew about."

Do you remember that experiment you did in elementary school where the teacher wanted to show you how mold or fungi grew? She wanted to demonstrate to you that mold spores are everywhere and you don't have to try too hard to find one. So she took a piece of bread, moistened it a little bit, and put it where? In the dark! In a warm, but dark, place. Yeast, mold, mildew and fungi always grow best in the dark. Once per year, the Jews clean their houses thoroughly in order to remove these agents from their houses. Why once per year? Because you don't have to try to catch a mold. It finds you. Likewise, a person of the light should periodically confess to the Father that he or she hasn't been perfect. Why? So that we won't lose our salvation? NO. So that we can be assured of heaven? NO. We need to throw out our yeast, clean off the light bulb that is the Holy Spirit so that we can stop play acting! If it is good for the home, it is good for the heart.

Finally, consider the words of the apostle John:

1 John 1:5b–9 [5b]God is light, and there is absolutely no darkness in Him. [6]If we say, "We have fellowship with Him," and walk in darkness, we are lying and are not practicing the truth. [7]But if we walk in the light as He Himself is in the light, we have fellowship with one another, and the blood of Jesus His Son cleanses us from all sin. [8]If we say, "We have no sin," we are deceiving ourselves, and the truth is not in us. [9]If we confess our sins, He is faithful and righteous to forgive us our sins and to cleanse us from all unrighteousness. *HCSB* [2]

Is your darkness passing away? Yes, we all have sinned. We mess up from time to time. But a Christian who is progressing in the faith should have less darkness in his heart today than you had this same time last year. This does not come from self-imposed discipline and reform like my Uncle Roy tried, but from the power of God to overcome the sin in your life. You can say you are in the light, but it is how you treat others that really demonstrates where you are. I've heard people say, "I love everybody" and then a minute later run down someone with their own mouth. It's hard to be in the light, with darkness coming out of your mouth. Your words are most often the best barometer of your heart. Is your darkness passing away? If not, it's time to confess and remove the yeast from your life. Let God's light shine forth in full. No more dusty 40 watt bulbs here!

Remember, when Jesus died for us, His atonement covered ALL our sin. Your past sin is all gone; the sin of today is all gone; the sin of tomorrow is like it never will happen. We just need to confess and possess what we've already been forgiven of. We need to live in the power Christ has over sin. If we're afraid to meet the needs of another because of what might be said about our past, forget it. Tell them God has forgiven you of it ALL. It still behooves us, now and then, to come and bend a knee before some altar, and confess to God "I've messed up", throw the leaven, the yeast, the fungus out; take out the 40 watts, put in the 100 watt.

However, confession has a more serious side to it. Do you remember this rule?:

Exodus 20:7 [7]You shall not misuse the name of the LORD your God, for the LORD will not hold anyone guiltless who misuses his name. NIV [4]

Thelma was adopted by a Kansas City physician who was a bachelor. With no mother in the house, she grew up a little resentful. As the years went on, she felt more and more bitter and acted out her frustrations on others at school. The day finally came when all her mischief caught up with her and she found herself in serious trouble. When her father arrived, he did his best to talk with the principal, and assure the school administrators his daughter would not behave in such a way again. Then, he took Thelma out in the hall and said, "I have given you my name. Live so that you don't ever bring shame to the name I've given you."

We have a merciful Father who has given us His holy name. In Acts 11:26, we read:

Acts 11:26c [26c]And the disciples were first called Christians in Antioch. NKJV [6]

The word *Christian* in the original Greek means "belonging to Messiah" or more commonly *little Messiah*. Confession, therefore, not only is an act of cleansing our heart, but of removing the stains we have put on His name. The rule of the Old Testament not only meant for people to literally reverence the name of God, but to live lives worthy of His name. Being a *little Messiah* should impact our lives radically. When do we quit being a *little Messiah*? At work? No. On the lake as we fish, or on the golf course? No. At home with the family? No. We are His representatives wherever we go. Sometimes, like Thelma and Uncle Roy, we may not be the best of ambassadors. But that can be changed through confession. In fact, that is what confession is all about—making things right with God again. After all, He is a Father of mercy. He is light and He desires that His light called Holy Spirit should shine brightly through all His *little Messiahs*.

If you have never experienced the mercy of the Father, or are not sure you have passed from darkness into the light, you can right now. See the appendix for help.

CHAPTER 4

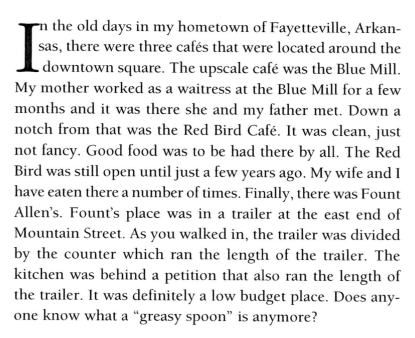

Fount Allen and a Father Who Is Real and Relevant

In the old days in my hometown of Fayetteville, Arkansas, there were three cafés that were located around the downtown square. The upscale café was the Blue Mill. My mother worked as a waitress at the Blue Mill for a few months and it was there she and my father met. Down a notch from that was the Red Bird Café. It was clean, just not fancy. Good food was to be had there by all. The Red Bird was still open until just a few years ago. My wife and I have eaten there a number of times. Finally, there was Fount Allen's. Fount's place was in a trailer at the east end of Mountain Street. As you walked in, the trailer was divided by the counter which ran the length of the trailer. The kitchen was behind a petition that also ran the length of the trailer. It was definitely a low budget place. Does anyone know what a "greasy spoon" is anymore?

One morning in the early to mid 1950's, my dad and my middle sister walked into Fount's for lunch. My sister was about seven at the time and ordered the same menu selection every time she could, no matter the restaurant or the town: a cheeseburger and chocolate milk. Fount was one of many practical jokers in town. Upon obtaining the usual order from my sister Priscilla, he set about doing his "work." Fount winked at my dad, so Dad knew something was up. Priscilla had no clue.

Fount went to work on the cheeseburgers. You could hear the grill sizzling, you could smell the meat cooking and see Fount going through all the motions of making a sandwich through the opening in the wall. When Fount brought out the cheeseburgers, he winked at Dad again and placed the orders in front of Priscilla and Dad.

Priscilla took a bite out of her burger. Lettuce, pickles, tomato, mustard and cheese. Mmm. She took another bite. Lettuce, pickles, tomato, mustard and cheese. Something was wrong here. She took one more gigantic bite by diving into the middle of the bun, as much as she could get into her mouth. Lettuce, pickles, tomato, mustard and cheese. She laid the burger down and lifted the top bun. No meat.

By this time Fount and Dad could hold their laughter no longer. Somehow it was funny watching Priscilla anxiously awaiting the satisfaction of a cheeseburger only to find she was eating the original veggie burger. Fount brought the meat patty out to Priscilla, apologized and spent the rest of the day chuckling.

Similar to the last chapter where we discussed letting as much of God's light shine through us as possible, this chapter deals with being relevant in a world of turmoil. To be blunt, do you want to eat a cheeseburger without meat?

If your answer is "no", then realize that most people in the darkness want to meet and know Christians that have substance. They want and need to meet an ambassador of God with pertinent answers to their questions. If such a person does not exist, in some cases people will turn to rules. The two fastest growing religions in the United States today (Islam and the Church of Jesus Christ of Latter Day Saints) are rules based cultures. Theirs are not loving, merciful gods, but gods of rules and laws. So then, how can we be sure we are people of substance as well as people of light so that the darkness walkers will be attracted to Christ? Perhaps we should know what substantive people are not. Consider the words of the apostle Paul:

> 2 Timothy 3:1–5 ¹But know this: difficult times will come in the last days. [The original Greek could also read "stressful times will come." Anyone stressed out lately?] ²For people will be lovers of self, lovers of money, boastful, proud, blasphemers, disobedient to parents, ungrateful, unholy, ³unloving, irreconcilable, slanderers, without self control, brutal, without love for what is good, ⁴traitors, reckless, conceited, lovers of pleasure rather than lovers of God, ⁵holding to the form of religion but denying its power. Avoid these people! HCSB ²

These verses paint a pretty bleak picture of the human race. Paul is definitely describing a people who have broken the rules. Isn't it interesting to note that these Scriptures appear to indicate that the source of stress and difficulty in the world is interacting with people who walk in darkness? Darkness walkers are selfish, lovers of money, find it difficult to reconcile and are ungrateful. Such people bring stress into our lives. It is easy to agree with this idea. However, the same idea implies that people who walk in the light have few, if any, of these attributes in their lives. Instead, light walkers are deeply concerned with the well-being of others, money is not their prime motivation, and they forgive easily and express gratitude. Why, then, are there so many who claim to walk in the light but have the attributes of those who walk in the dark? There are two reasons. First, some true light walkers have yet to remove their dark corners as discussed in the previous chapter. The second answer is found in verse five where Paul says, "holding to a form of religion [other translations have godliness] but denying its power." Paul says that, like Fount Allen's cheeseburger with no meat, many people are just window dressing with no real joy or godliness in their lives. They are religious, but don't know Jesus Christ. You meet people like this every day. Cheeseburgers with no meat, religious people who obey many rules, yet they are without God.

I am sure that your reaction to my illustration of a religious person being a cheeseburger with no meat is something to the effect: "This is the silliest thing I've ever read in my life." And you're right. Do you want to know what is sillier than this illustration? Calling yourself a person of light and yet having attitudes and actions that mirror darkness (selfishness, greed, ingratitude, conceit . . .). Now that's silly. The good news is that silliness and ignorance can be overcome.

The sad part about life is that people without God, the darkness walkers, are looking for the real thing. Like the old advertisement, they yell out "Where's the beef?" and too many times, we who call ourselves light, let them down. Instead of telling them of God's love, we burden them with rules. Instead of showing them God's love, we lecture them. If Holy Spirit is in our lives, we should be a conduit of that light that is moldable to meet the needs of others. To illustrate my point, let's look at another story.

Dale grew up on a farm just north of Lincoln, Nebraska in the community of Davy. A trunk line of the Chicago and Northwestern railroad bisected his father's farm. During the days of the depression, there were a number of "hobos" who walked the track going to Lincoln and they would stop at the house and ask for handouts. Dale said his father would seldom, if ever; give the hobos anything but a face full of door. But then one day, something very different happened.

It was in the late spring during winter wheat harvest. The weather had not been cooperative, so the harvest was late coming out of the field. Dale and his father had worked many days of long hours and still they were far behind. Early one morning as they prepared to enter the wheat field again, they noticed walking down the railroad track was a Native American man and his family (a wife and three half grown children). Not giving it much thought, they proceeded on to the wheat field. As they fired up the thrasher, they heard a man's voice.

"You need help? We work for pay."

They turned around to find the Indian family standing there in the field with their heads held high. Dale said his father was somewhat surprised because they wanted work and not a hand out.

"Have you harvested wheat before?"

The man didn't reply, he just grabbed the reins of the horses pulling the mower and started cutting wheat. His wife and children would gather the wheat and run it to the thrasher where Dale and his dad worked. Dale said he, a farm boy, never saw people work so hard in his entire life. By mid afternoon it was very apparent that the wheat harvest would be completed that day. With this knowledge, Dale's father slipped off to the house. There, he had his wife prepare a large feast of fried chicken and ham with all the trimmings for the evening meal.

Sure enough, just at dusk, the wheat harvest was in. The grain was stored safely away and the straw was all bundled. Dale's father approached the Indian man and asked, "Besides pay, I want you and your family to eat with us tonight" and he pointed towards the farmhouse.

"No," came the reply, "No go in white man's house. You pay, we go." The look on the Indian's face told the whole story. He was very definitely not going into any white man's dwelling. But Dale knew his father was just as stubborn and that the man and his family would share a meal. At this point, Dale's father had a decision to make. Do I force them into my home or come up with another idea?

"Come here, son." Dale followed his father to the house where they removed the dining room table and all the chairs and placed them under a large tree in the front yard. There, Dale's mom served the meal and everyone ate together. Dale was proud that his father had such a stroke of genius. This was especially so because it appeared that it had been some time since the Indian children had had anything to eat as they ate their meal very fast. After the meal, the family accepted a dollar or two and then moved on down the railroad track towards Lincoln.

Dale's father had several chances during this episode to walk selfishly. When the Indian offered to help, he could have said no. When the Indian took control of his implement and began to cut the wheat, he could have grabbed it away from the man and said, "I'll do that." When the Indian refused to enter his house, he could have been offended and said, "Well, I offered." But time and again he was willing to let go of self and, in so doing, to reach out to someone else. To be relevant to a dark society, in order NOT to be a cheeseburger without meat, we need to follow the example of Dale's father and extend ourselves to touch the lives of others. We need to accept and love them as they are. Furthermore, the people of light should offer to the world those things which have eternal value and not mirror what the world teaches is important. Money has no value in eternity. Pleasure is soon forgotten on earth, let alone has any meaning in eternity. Grudges and bitterness end when the person who harbors those feelings dies. The things which last eternally, which the Bible refers to as "gold", are first of all, our decision to follow Jesus Christ;

second, the magnitude of how we've invested our lives into other people and similarly how we've influenced other people by our words and actions. All else is short lived. Consider another passage written by the Apostle Paul:

> 1 Corinthians 3:9, 11–15 [9] For we are God's fellow workers; you are God's field, God's building ⋯ [11] For no one can lay any foundation other than the one already laid, which is Jesus Christ. [12] If any man builds on this foundation using gold, silver, costly stones, wood, hay or straw, [13] his work will be shown for what it is, because the Day [referring to a Christian's judgment before Christ] will bring it to LIGHT. It will be revealed with fire, and the fire will test the quality of each man's work. [14] If what he has built survives, he will receive his reward. [15] If it is burned up, he will suffer loss; he himself will be saved, but only as one escaping through the flames. *NIV* [4] (emphasis added)

Here the apostle compares doing things eternal to building construction. Every event that we hope will be eternal, every word given to another human being; every action is laid upon some foundation. For the people who walk in darkness, their foundation might be their own intellect or self will. It could be a belief in the New Age tenants of pantheism, monism and reincarnation. Finally, it might be a belief in a religious system. But note what the apostle said. There is only one true foundation that will last through eternity and that foundation is Jesus Christ. It doesn't matter what you've been told or fervently believe, there is no other foundation other than Jesus, and all other religious activity is futile. To recite memorized prayers without knowing the God who hears is futile. To perform religious acts without feeling is futile. But when you have and know Jesus, you possess the universe.

For those who've come to the light, we build our eternal things upon Christ. Some build with costly material. Some build with poor material. If we are not similar to Dale's father in that we overcome cultural and spiritual barriers to present light to a dark world, then our working amounts to firewood. If what motivates us to work towards things that we consider eternal is money, pleasure or the assurance our name will last forever and not the name of Christ, then those works are firewood. (Consider that firewood is very temporary. It exists to be destroyed. The things of this world are temporary and extremely flammable in the presence of God). Notice I didn't say the work itself. It is the motivation of why we do a work that is important. To render a work with the wrong motivation is to be a cheeseburger without meat. It looks good on the outside, but it is empty from within. In a greater sense then, we are acting out the role of a worker of good (anyone remember the definition of hypocrite?) and as such we really are only trying to deceive the world. At this realization, we should also remember who is called the father of lies and the Deceiver and comprehend whose team we've just scored for. Not God's. Thus, our goal is to be so filled with Holy Spirit as to let the very existence of Christ be who we are. When our dark corners are removed, when we cast off the attitudes and deceptions of this world, we will be like Christ. Being transparent and real at that point is no longer a challenge because we act and speak as Holy Spirit directs.

How, then, can we know if we are building upon the foundation of Christ with gold or just making firewood? Look closely at verse nine in the passage above. If we look around our life and Christ is building with us, we're making gold. If we look around and notice we are all alone, we're just chopping firewood. God is our co-builder when gold is made. You chop firewood alone.

When the deception of Fount Allen's was over, my sister Priscilla obtained a cheeseburger with meat. How long until you are genuine in your faith without holding on to this temporal world? How long will you hold on to what the world says is important (self, money and pleasure) and mirror the world instead of changing the world from darkness to light? How long will you work towards the temporary and let the truly eternal pass? One more hour is too long. You may try to act out the role of a light walker, but those who walk in the darkness see you for who you really are: a silly cheeseburger with no meat. Be real. Be genuine. Be Spirit led. Why? Because being led by the Spirit just blows the world away. They have nothing to match it.

If you are not sure that you have passed from darkness into light, if you have tired of the phoniness of religion, there is a way you can know the living and true God. See the end of the book for help.

CHAPTER 5

Being a Mirror of the Father's Love

Flossy and Otto ran the "mom and pop" grocery store in our neighborhood. My parents would often stop by their store, and I would tag along. Mom or Dad would buy their boy a soda pop or some candy. As I remember Flossy and Otto, they were an older couple in the early 1960's and I am not sure they ever had any children. Their store was the social center of our then small community because they only sold gasoline, candy, soda pop and luncheon meats. If you wanted more than that, you had to drive into town. But if you wanted what they had to sell as well as social interaction with the community, Flossy and Otto's was the place to be.

Like my parents, Flossy and Otto were Baptist by denomination. Not the same stripe of Baptist, but Baptist. They attended the Buckner Freewill Baptist Church every Sunday, their health permitting, for more than forty years. Since they were storeowners, Otto could afford to buy a nice car to drive Flossy to church—a Chrysler Imperial. At 9:30 sharp every Sunday morning, their Imperial would head out of their driveway and turn east for the short drive to Buckner.

One particular Sunday, Otto said he got into the car as always, started the engine and started talking to Flossy. He talked to her all the way to church. He talked to her all the way into the church doors. But when he arrived at their Sunday School room, Flossy was nowhere to be found. "Well," he thought to himself, "she must be watching the nursery today." So he walked down to the nursery. No Flossy. "She must have decided to attend the pastor's class today" he muttered to himself. He walked up the stairs to the sanctuary. No Flossy. Her coat was not hanging in the vestibule. Where did Flossy go?

At long last, Otto decided to retrace his steps. He got back into his Imperial and drove home. By this time, worry had so consumed him that he began to sweat. Being in such a state of anxiety, it was hard to drive. But finally, he pulled into the driveway and got out of his car. Sure enough, he found Flossy—sitting on the front porch. She had been waiting half an hour for Otto to come home and pick her up.

Just as Otto took Flossy for granted, there is much about the Christian life we take for granted as well. Take love for example. The world as a whole gives a bunch of lip service to love, but few people really understand the word. Remember the Scripture from chapter one where Isaiah wrote:

Isaiah 29:13 [13] The Lord says: 'These people come near to me with their mouth and honor me with their lips, but their hearts are far from me.' *NIV* [4]

Most dictionaries will list the word "love" as both a noun and a verb. They will try to define the word with such terms as "deep emotion" or "feelings of affection." They will tell you that sexual intercourse is "making love." All of these, as Isaiah stated, dance around the issue of what true biblical love is all about. Biblical love has nothing at all to do with one's feelings. Biblical love has everything to do with your character, your attitudes and your actions. Consider very carefully the words of Jesus found in the Gospel of John:

John 15:12 [12] This is My commandment, that you love one another as I have loved you. *NKJV* [6]

Remember what we said in chapter two about commandments? They are God's standards for our behavior. Most of the time, we cannot live up to His standards. However, they do give us a glimpse of how God expects us to act. Therefore, it is a pretty good idea to understand the rule above so that we will know what is expected of us. We will not be able to keep this rule all our lives, but God is a God of grace and He understands.

"Love one another as I have loved you." Here again, when we fully understand what Jesus is saying, our ability to obey this rule is almost nil. But with the aid of Holy Spirit, God is able to work through us so we can be mirrors or conduits of His love and concern. How did Jesus love His disciples? He gave of Himself. He shared. He delegated authority. He spent time with them. While superior to His disciples, He was not conceited. None of these have anything to do with emotions or feelings; they are actions and the attitudes behind those actions. Most of us in today's American society allow ourselves to be so over-scheduled that we have little time left in a day to love others as Jesus did. We throw up our hands and simply say that we don't have the time. It takes time to give of yourself. It takes time to share with someone else. "Above all, don't think for one minute that when I've actually obtained a little authority in my life over others that I am going to give that away. I've worked hard to get to where I am," so we tell ourselves. In thinking this way, we reveal our attitude about love. And thus, with our excuses, we've failed to live up to the standard of God before we even try. Like Otto, we take for granted that which we say we prize the most. How then, is love put into action?

It was one of the worst thunderstorms I had ever seen. I could hardly see past the hood of the car as I drove down Interstate 80 across western Iowa. The voice on the radio kept announcing tornado warnings for towns all around me, but I pressed on. On through the rain, the wind, the lightening and on to Ellsworth.

As a service to the local farmers, every spring the University of Nebraska Poultry Farm would buy day-old baby turkeys (called poults), raise them for a few weeks in order to cull out the sick ones, and then sell them to the farmers as "started poults." In turn, the locals would raise the turkeys to market weight and sell them as fresh turkeys during the Thanksgiving season. Thus, the locals made money, the poultry farm made money and the hatchery made money. What the business world calls a "win-win situation." The only problem this year was that our normal hatchery was sold out of poults, so I had to drive to a hatchery in Ellsworth, Iowa and bring the baby turkeys back to Lincoln.

Passing car after car that had drowned out or that had stopped due to poor visibility, I drove on around Des Moines, up Interstate 35 North, passed Ames and finally to Ellsworth. As I pulled up to the hatchery, the rain was falling as hard as ever. I waited for a moment to see if the rain would let up. Not a chance. Nothing to do but run for it. I opened the door to the station wagon, jumped out and made a dash for the front door. Running without a coat, I was drenched when I entered the lobby.

"What on earth are you doing here?" was the greeting I received from the hatchery manager when I stopped to shake the water off my hair. "You must be crazy to be out in this weather!"

"Not crazy, sir, just from Nebraska."

Turning to his secretary, he called out, "Linda, get this boy a towel. He's soaked!"

After a few moments, a terry cloth towel was covering my head, a soda pop was placed in my hand and deep down inside I had sense of relief that I had stumbled into such a welcoming place.

"Now, just why is it you're here?" he asked.

"I'm from the University of Nebraska, sir. I've come for our poult order."

"Let me go check on them. I'll be right back."

Taking a sip from the soda, I once again realized what a warm, welcoming place this was. Not fancy. Just homey. The manager really seemed to go out of his way to look after me. And then I saw the sign. After seeing the sign, I knew why I sensed so much goodness in the place on this day. The sign read something to the effect: "If you've met me, you've met no one. But if you've missed meeting Jesus, you've missed everything."

Here was a man that had some light in him. Even if I hadn't seen the sign, I probably would have guessed he was a person of light. Why? Because on this stormy, nasty day he treated a wet, goofy college boy with dignity and respect—almost as you would a son. I knew he was a person of light not because of what he was or how he felt, but because of what he did and the attitude of concern he had. Soon the station wagon was loaded and I was headed back to Lincoln. As I drove I was thankful to God He had put such a caring person on my pathway that day. I was there at the hatchery for only a few moments, but they are moments I will never forget.

Here then are a few glimpses of truth: It can be evident whether or not you are of the light simply by what you do and the attitude with which you do it. We are mirrors of the Father's love and it is very apparent how closely we've been walking with Him by our actions and attitudes. How

I treat others is directly related to my relationship to the Father. To treat others with love, I have to know that I am loved myself. Unfortunately, like Otto, we take these truths for granted all too often.

To illustrate my point, consider closely the words of the Apostle Paul:

> 1 Corinthians 13:1–7 [1]If I could speak in any language in heaven or on earth but didn't love others, I would only be making meaningless noise like a loud gong or a clanging cymbal. [2]If I had the gift of prophecy, and if I knew all the mysteries of the future and knew everything about everything, but didn't love others, what good would I be? And if I had the gift of faith so that I could speak to a mountain and make it move, without love I would be no good to anybody. [3]If I gave everything I have to the poor and even sacrificed my body, I could boast about it; but if I didn't love others, I would be of no value whatsoever.
>
> [4]Love is patient and kind. Love is not jealous or boastful or proud [5]or rude. Love does not demand its own way. Love is not irritable, and it keeps no record of when it has been wronged. [6]It is never glad about injustice but rejoices whenever the truth wins out. [7]Love never gives up, never loses faith, is always hopeful, and endures through every circumstance. *NLT* [3]

First, Paul addresses the attitudes we have about ourselves. Most of us who have a college degree or two spend the rest of our lives trying to impress others with our intellect. We take pride in being able, perhaps, to speak another language other than our native tongue or to solve complicated and convoluted problems with reason and deduction. We enter politics or the public arena with an attitude of "I know what's best for you." Having a sense of self worth is a good thing, but not if we base that on temporary, earthly things. Paul states that if I were able to speak several languages, and were able to predict the future and have a great deal of intellectual knowledge, but don't love others, I become of no value. He didn't say I have little value, he said I would have no value (verse 3). Therefore, my sense of self worth should not be based on what I am, but who I am. Our heavenly Father gave all He had, all He ever hoped to obtain, in the form of Jesus. Jesus was executed and resurrected so that I might know how much the Father loves me. I am His adopted child, the adopted son of the living, Most High God. Knowing this, I should be able to use my intellect and the other gifts God has given me to mirror the Father's love to others.

Paul goes on to make another point. If I had a great deal of money and did something very religious with it by giving it away, that act of service would be worthless if I didn't do it with an attitude of love. Riches are seen by some as a sign of God's blessing on your life. If God has blessed you, they believe, you will have money. The other view of wealth is that a good Christian must take a vow of poverty in order to be Christ-like. Since both of these views are so extreme, it should be obvious that both miss the point and the real truth will lie somewhere in the middle. Whether my gift comes from a full purse or an empty one is somewhat irrelevant. If my gift comes from a loveless heart and attitude, the apostle says it is worthless, regardless of size. Not useless. Worthless. If my gift, however small or great, comes from a loving attitude, then something eternal has been accomplished.

Finally, the apostle Paul says that if I am a religious person, so full of faith that what seems impossible to man suddenly becomes reality, but without exercising my faith in love, I amount to nothing. My faith is worthless. Not only would I be a cheeseburger without meat, but I join Otto in taking the greatest force of the universe for granted. Here then is a terrible truth: you can be a very religious, faith-filled person and yet practice that faith without love. We shouldn't be shocked about this because it happens every day. Not only is it occurring in the present, but this condition has gone on for thousands of years. The children of Israel were God's chosen people to be a light unto their world. In the Old Testament we read that they were too busy worshipping fertility idols to be God's light.[A] In the time of Jesus, the Jews were too busy trying to stay holy and to separate themselves from Roman society to be God's light. Now that we are in the church age, each Christian must ask, "Am I being so religious and so busy obeying rules that I am failing to mirror God's love?" Moving moun-

---

[A] The worship of fertility gods dealt mostly with the Hebrews' lack of faith in God to provide for them. Fertility gods promised bountiful harvests of wheat and grapes, abundant livestock reproduction and thus, full wallets. The means by which these idols were to be worshipped involved promiscuous sex and child sacrifice. This will be important to remember in later chapters.

tains by faith is great, but if it fails to meet the needs of people in a dark world, it is worthless. Not useless. Worthless.

Right now in my pocket I have several keys that I can't remember which locks on what door they belong to. Some keys, I know for certain, the locks have been moved from the doors they used to open. What are those keys? For the time being, useless. But if I find the lock they open, they at that point will have value. Being temporarily unused by God is okay. Being declared worthless by God is a nightmare. Much better then, to be useless than worthless. Useless can be changed. Worthless is permanent.

The apostle Paul goes on to describe the attributes of a person who loves.

Love is patient and kind. Wouldn't things between Flossy and Otto have turned out better if Otto had truly waited for Flossy to announce she was ready to go to church? Instead, when the clock struck 9:30, Otto assumed Flossy was ready, jumped in the Imperial and headed down the road. Patience would have waited until the other person was ready. Kindness would have dictated that the other person's needs came first. Time would have mattered little. Too often, we are like Otto and let the clock run our lives instead of patience. Kindness was what was shown to me by the manager of the hatchery. He took the time to care for my needs instead of letting the clock run his life.

Love is not jealous or boastful or proud or rude. Jealousy, pride and just plain being stuck up are sure signs

66

that we have a few dark corners in our hearts to remove and that the light within us is weak. Jealousy, pride and rudeness all stem from a self-centered view of the world. "For the world to be right, I must be the center of all that goes on around me." Pride, in and of itself, denotes that the person considers his or her intellect to be superior to God's. Such an attitude illuminates just how ignorant they really are. We may be able to remember the past and the lessons we learned there. We may even be able to control those around us in the present. But God sees the future, and we cannot know the next moment. A true light giver and mirror of God's love is not self centered, but God centered. All in the world will be right if HE (God) is the center of attention.

Love is not irritable, and it keeps no record of when it has been wronged. If you still remember that wonderful gift you gave so and so for Christmas thirteen years ago and that you've never received a thank you card or even a return gift the next Christmas, then you are not dealing with that person in love. If you can remember every time so and so put you down verbally, then you are not dealing with that person in love. Love demands that we forgive and forget what is past and let God hand out judgment when and if judgment is due. If every time a loved one speaks to us and we give a harsh answer, we are not dealing with that person in love. Love is not irritable. Love considers what is best to say before the mouth engages in speech.

Love never gives up, never loses faith, is always hopeful, and endures through every circumstance. Having God at the center of our universe is never disappointing. Loving a people filled with darkness will always lead to disappointment. Since we all have at least a little darkness in our hearts, since we tend to mess up, we also let each other down. When that happens, the apostle says never give up on whoever let you down. Never lose faith in them. Always have hope that they will confess, repent and turn to God. This may take a great deal of time and so he says we should endure through every circumstance. Not trot through the situation merrily. Endure. One of the great shortfalls of Christians of the twenty-first century in the western world is that we don't know how to endure. We've never been taught to endure. Endurance does not come at the end of a remote control. It takes time.

How can I tell if I'm loving people? If you are full of self pride, irritable, short on time and patience, you are not walking in love. Few people have been an example to me of mirroring the love of God to others. But here is a fine example:

Most people consider Fairland, Oklahoma just a wide place in the road. The Burlington Northern Railroad and U.S. Highway 60 pass through town and most people that arrive in Fairland do too. However, like most small towns in this nation, there is more to Fairland than one would expect as you drive past. Fairland has 1,000 people, and thus 1,000 ways to potentially change eternity. On this particular day, my friend George was trying to do just that.

The little blue truck that George owned rolled down the dusty road just outside of Fairland, Oklahoma. Inside the cab were my friend George and me. We were on our way to visit a man who had not been to church for some time. As we rolled on, George explained to me the reasons behind this man's lack of attendance.

It was years ago when this man was a faithful member and attendee of the church. Unfortunately, his wife left him for another man in the church and this man's whole life was shattered. George was uncertain how we would be received, as it had been a number of years since anyone from the church had been to see him. It was rumored that the man had remarried, but no one knew for sure. George went on to explain the heartache that is caused when the people of light live in a thousand shades of gray instead of mirroring the light and love of God.

The little blue truck crossed over Grand River and passed huge oak and sycamore trees as we drove towards a humble house on the edge of a field. As we pulled into the yard next to the house, a tall, broad shouldered man with hands as big as baseball mitts walked out of the house and toward the little blue truck.

"Let me do most of the talking," George instructed as we got out of the truck. "Hello stranger, do you remember me?" George asked.

For a few moments, the eyes of the man looked a little blank as he searched his memory for the short, stocky man that just greeted him. Then, when memories finally flooded his mind, I saw tears roll down the big man's cheek. Short, stocky George went over and put his arms around the big man and for a few moments, they wept together.

"We sure have missed seeing you at church," George told the man.

"I know," the man replied as he wiped tears off his face, "but there are just too many bad memories in that place. I don't know if I could ever go back. The last time I was there, all I could see was images of her. And him."

About this time a young woman appeared at the door and called out to the man, "Who are you visiting with?"

The man replied, "Come here, honey, I want you to meet someone."

As she exited the house, she appeared to be a good 15 to 20 years younger than the man we came to see and perhaps not much older than I was.

"George, I'd like for you to meet my new wife. George is from the church. And this young fellar is . . ."

"Paul. My name is Paul. Good to meet you both."

"To be honest, George, she is the other reason I'm not sure I can ever go back to that church. I'm just not sure how the people would accept or treat her."

George never batted an eye, but stood there patiently and listened to the man's story. "Well I certainly understand how you feel, but I hate that it has to be that way." After a short silence, George went on to say, "I just want to remind you that the Lord loves you and I do as well. I think it would be best for the both of you if attended church somewhere."

The big man just nodded his head.

After a handshake, George and I returned to the little blue truck, left the humble house and headed back to Fairland. It occurred to me on the way back to town that to be a mirror of God's light and love, you must not only observe to love those who walk in darkness, but also to take time to care for the wounded inside the household of faith as well. Too often the needs of the wounded go unmet when just a hug and some patient listening will go a long way to demonstrate how much the Father loves us.

However, being a mirror of God's love goes beyond the boundaries of the church. The principle also applies where you work.

I was riding along with the president of a food company from Texas that grows and finishes their own chickens. It is a very large organization that owns hatcheries, feed mills and food processing plants. I felt very honored to be taking a short tour of the facilities with this man on this particular day when the following events took place. The man with whom I was tagging along was my brother-in-law, Bob, and this particular day was Thanksgiving Day of 1990.

As we toured some of the newer buildings, Bob and I heard a dull, almost thunderous sound coming from the feed mill. Bob drove around the building to find a man

71

trying to unload a railroad car full of soybean meal.[B] To accomplish the unloading, the man had to beat the side of the car with a sledgehammer. With each strike of the sledge, only traces of meal would fall from the trap doors on the bottom of the car. Being intent on his work, he didn't notice as Bob and I pulled up in the truck to the unloading area.

BOOM . . . BOOM . . . BOOM was the steady pace of the hammer striking the car.

"Hey Tom!" Bob yelled.

The man jumped and missed hitting the railroad car.

"Oh, hello sir."

"Getting ready for tomorrow?"

"Yeah, I'm trying to stay one step ahead."

"That's good. How's that girl of yours? Did she ever get over her sickness?"

"Yessir, she's out of the hospital now."

[B] So that you can fully understand what's going on here, know that soybean meal is the primary protein supplement in all poultry and swine feeds. It is delivered in hopper bottom rail cars to the mills that manufacture feed. Because the meal is a flaked material similar to oatmeal, a great deal of settling occurs during transport. I have personally witnessed an event where the railroad car would cross the scales weighing 100 tons, opening the top hatch revealed the car was full of meal, yet when the bottom trap door was opened, nothing would fall out.

"Well that's wonderful. Know that we'll keep praying for her."

"Thank you, sir."

"Well, we'll be running along. Sorry we scared you."

And with that, Bob rolled up the window on the truck and we moved along. But did you notice what just happened? The president and CEO of this company knew the name of the hourly employee that was paid to beat railroad cars. Not only did Bob know his name, he knew details about the man's family, that he had a daughter who had been ill. Moreover, he had been praying for her recovery. How many CEO's do you know of that remember the names of their "grunt" employees, let alone details about their lives? I know just one. If you are an employer, how often do you pray for your employees? I'm sure you pray for zero worker's compensation claims. But do you really pray and show God's light and love to your employees?

If you happen to be on the other end of the spectrum, how often do you pray for your boss and the officers of your company? Twice a year? Once a year? Never? Face it, most of us are just grateful that our paychecks don't bounce, let alone be concerned for the "fat cat" who is driving the nice company car. Employers showing concern for employees and employees showing genuine concern for their employers are both mirrors of God's love. It doesn't happen in many places, but it should.

Unlike the people of light who have God and the church for moral support, the people who are of the darkness only have their co-workers and friends as a support mechanism. Thus, in some places, there tends to be a lot of sharing about family issues. If you happen to be employed at a company where there is the opportunity for interaction, thank God that you have the chance to mirror God's light. Unlike Otto, don't take this for granted. Notice those around you who have an ear to hear about Jesus and invest your time into them.

The greatest gift Otto was given in his life was his wife Flossy. Yet one day he exhibited so little interest in her, he drove away in his Imperial and left her sitting on the porch. Years later, after Flossy developed Alzheimers disease, he cared for her every need and waited upon her 24 hours a day, seven days a week until she died. His devotion to her was such that, just two weeks after she left this world, he too went home to meet the Lord. They say he died of natural causes, I assumed Otto died of a broken heart.

The greatest gift a Christian is given is the opportunity to mirror the light and love of God to a dark world. We should skillfully use this gift when we meet customers as the man in Ellsworth, Iowa did, when we deal with employees or employers on the job as my relative Bob did, or trying to reclaim and heal a wounded brother in Christ as my friend George did. However, the only way you obtain this gift is to pass from darkness to light. If you are not sure you have ever done this, please see the appendix for help.

CHAPTER 6

A Father of Peace

T ickets please," the new conductor repeated as he came down the aisle of the railroad car. Passengers were reaching into purses, wallets and coat pockets to hand over their tickets for hole punching.

"He's bigger than the last two," the logger thought to himself, "but he can still be taken down. Plenty of others on this car to help me do it. After all, we have the right to ride this train for free. If it weren't for us, this tar bucket wouldn't make any money at all."

"Tickets please." The new conductor was coming closer, just a few seats away from the logger.

"Wooooeee. Look at the arms on that fella. He almost looks like he's ran a few crosscut saws himself."

Finally, the conductor approached the logger's seat.

"Ticket please."

"Ain't got none. Don't want any."

"Listen buster, everybody has to have a ticket. No free loaders."

"I ain't no free loader. I'm the only reason this railroad makes any money. See those logs on them thar flat cars back yonder? I'm the reason they're there."

"I don't care if you're a preacher, if you don't have a ticket, you don't ride."

With that, the logger jumped up and grabbed the conductor by the coat with his left hand and cocked his right arm back and prepared to deliver the first blow.

"Fight! Fight!" passengers yelled through the car as men jumped on their seats to see the carnage and women grabbed their children for fear of them being hurt in the brawl.

Welcome to what is officially known as the Fayetteville and Little Rock railroad or as the natives called it "the Saint Paul line." Completed in 1886, purchased by the Frisco railroad in 1887, this trunk line runs just 35 miles southeast from Fayetteville to the logging and lumber town of Saint Paul, Arkansas. Trees felled around Saint Paul were either milled into railroad ties in town, or the logs were taken to Fulbright's lumber mill in Fayetteville and turned into hardwood flooring and other hardwood lumber. Every morning for 30 years, the train would make its way from Fayetteville through the tree-laden hills to Saint Paul pulling empty flat cars, a mail car and a passenger car or two for those wanting to make the trip. In the evening, the train would make its way back from Saint Paul hauling ties, logs, mail and what few passengers that wanted to ride into the city.

Here of late, though, the rough men that cut the trees and milled the timber insisted on riding to Fayetteville for free. Their logic was that, since it was the timber that made the rail line money, and since the cut timber wouldn't exist if not for them, they should get a free pass. Of course, they failed to check with the railroad first. Since the loggers started this scheme, two, and possibly three, conductors had been thrown off the train by physical force. Old, skinny conductors had a tough time fighting two to three big, husky loggers. This day, however, things would be different.

Likewise, I would like to introduce you to my father's boyhood hero, Mr. George McQueen. Mr. McQueen was my father's uncle by marriage. Tall, broad shouldered and with huge biceps, he was the equal of any logger. That is why the Frisco railroad hired him on as conductor and gave him strict orders against loggers and lumbermen riding for free. Until my father was way up in years, he insisted that every episode of the television series Gunsmoke or any John Wayne western movie was somehow based on the life of George McQueen. To my father, Mr. McQueen was a real, larger than life champion of justice. We will soon see if the Frisco railroad was insightful in hiring Mr. McQueen for this job.

"Get'm boys!" the logger yelled as his fist landed across Mr. McQueen's jaw. Two other men of the woods stood up to join in the fight. But unlike previous brawls, this one was now different. Instead of a frail old man lying on the floor of the railroad car to be kicked and beaten, this guy had just been knocked backwards a couple of steps and now he looked angry.

"Are you boys sure you want to start this?" Mr. McQueen asked as he grabbed one of the men by the coat collar and began dragging him past his friends to the back door.

Seeing their friend being removed from the train, the two remaining loggers jumped Mr. McQueen, one using a small stick of firewood to strike him on the head. But the blows bounced off the new conductor like raindrops bouncing off a roof.

"You boys keep this up and I'm liable to get mad," Mr. McQueen calmly stated as the first logger disappeared from the rear platform of the train into the brush along the tracks.

"Which one of you wants to be next?"

Looking at each other with eyes full of amazement, the two remaining loggers each jumped out of a window to avoid the inevitable. The men standing in their seats to see a fight quickly sat down. The women hovering over their children to protect them from the fray now sat upright with wide smiles on their faces. Peace had finally arrived on the Saint Paul line and it remained so until the line was shut down in 1937. In fact, the town council of Saint Paul was so impressed with the exploits of Mr. McQueen, they hired him away from the railroad and appointed him Town Marshall for a time. Other stories can be told here of the peacemaking abilities of Mr. McQueen, but perhaps they are best saved for another time. A year or so later, Aunt Laura and her husband, Mr. McQueen, moved to Tahlequah, Oklahoma and lived quiet, but happy lives.

While the above is an extreme example of peacemaking, the Bible calls upon each of us to be peacemakers. While the example I've given is one of physical violence to bring peace, the battle a Christian is called upon to fight is much more serious. It is a spiritual battle. Thus, while we all should denounce and avoid violence, we should likewise realize that spiritual warfare can be as demanding as physical pursuits, if not more so. While violence tends to produce more violence, the ultimate end of a spiritual battle is peace. The apostle Matthew wrote:

> Matthew 5:9 ⁹Blessed [some translations read 'Happy'] are the peacemakers, because they will be called sons of God. HCSB[2]

When most people read these words, they think of Henry Kissinger and his attempts to bring peace to war-torn Vietnam and the Middle East. Or they may remember Neville Chamberlin, the prime minister of Great Britain before World War II, and his famous declaration "I have spoken with Heir Hitler and hold in my hand the paper bearing his signature that guarantees us peace in our time." Finally, they may think of such a person as Mr. McQueen, who through some force or violence, brought about peace. All of these preconceptions of what a peacemaker should be are entirely wrong. The peacemaker the Bible refers to is not a negotiator, a pacifist, or a person of violence. The spiritual battle we are called upon to wage usually just involves two parties—you and God. The peace we are called upon to secure is not between nations, but between you and God, you and your past, you and your fellow children of light.

The writer of the book of Hebrews explains this principle:

> Hebrews 12:14–16 [14]Pursue peace with everyone, and holiness—without it no one will see the Lord. [15]See to it that no one falls short of the grace of God and that no root of bitterness springs up, causing trouble and by it, defiling many. [16]And see that there isn't any immoral or irreverent person like Esau, who sold his birthright in exchange for one meal. *HCSB* [2]

First of all, we should pursue peace between ourselves and God. When there is peace between us and God, the natural outcome of this is that we will be holy. Because we are holy, we will see God and where He is at work on this earth as well as seeing Him in heaven.

If today you can't remember a time when you invited Jesus into your heart and life, being a peacemaker means you stop doing things on your own and let God take control of your life. To be at peace with God, you need holiness. Being holy is something we humans can't do on our own. We need what theologians call justification. That is, being holy before God. Justification comes from passing from darkness into light and happens immediately when that transformation takes place.

Christian, are you moving towards holiness? Theologians call that sanctification. Final sanctification will come from God. Until then, we need to strive to be a holy people. Pure. Without spot. To be a peacemaker with God, you need to be holy. However, there are a number of stumbling blocks that the Deceiver puts in our way.

Being motivated by materialism is the first of these stumbling blocks. The writer of Hebrews tells us to remember Esau. He was a man who sold all his privileges as first born to his twin brother. What did he obtain in return for such a high price? A bowl of soup. A silly bowl of soup. At the moment, that bowl of soup looked, smelled and tasted really good. Later on, Esau realized he had made a poor bargain.

One of the greatest threats to the twenty-first century church in the United States is not outside interference by government or some other faith, but our greed to obtain the things this world offers. I am not saying we should all take a vow of poverty. What I am saying is that if our whole theology is wrapped up in God giving us THINGS instead of HIMSELF, the writer of Hebrews calls us immoral and irreverent. What a terrible place to be. We should value our walk with God more than any object, position or amount of money. God does not necessarily reward the holy with things, but He would rather reward the holy with more of Himself. It is a very Pharisee-like manner of thinking to believe God rewards holiness with the stuff this world offers when holiness is a reward in and of itself. Do you remember the footnote in chapter five about why the Jews worshipped fertility gods? Was it not because they wanted full wallets? We would be wise, then, to remember their folly and not repeat it. Much of the advice the Old Testament man Job received from his friends was junk. But listen closely to the words of Eliphaz:

> Job 22:21–25 [21]Submit to God and be at peace with him; in this way prosperity will come to you. [22]Accept instruction from his mouth and lay up his words in your heart. [23] If you return to the Almighty, you will be restored: If you remove wickedness far from your tent [24]and assign your nuggets to the dust, your gold of Ophir to the rocks in the ravines, [25]then the Almighty will be your gold, the choicest silver for you. *NIV* [4]

Does God want us poor? No. Does God want us all filthy rich? No. What God desires is for us to consider Him better than gold or silver. Being poor is not a sign you have failed God. Being rich is not a sign God is overly pleased with you. Being holy and knowing that He is better for me than gold is God's prosperity for my soul. If you have a lot of stuff, glorify God with it. Are you poor? Glorify God. Be a peacemaker with God.

Does pornography have your attention? If you can answer yes, you're neither holy nor a peacemaker with God. Pornography is another huge threat to the twenty-first century church. Here the Deceiver thinks he has us where we won't let go because we are "wired" to find the opposite sex attractive. Yet pornography perverts this natural attraction and, after a time, we feel that sex is nasty instead of the God-given, wholesome thing it is between a husband and a wife. Pornography not only exploits the women who put themselves on display, but also exploits the men who stare at those images that will be so difficult for them to forget. Because those images linger in the mind of a man for so long, it strains the relationship we have with God. However, the promise of God's Word above in verses twenty-three and twenty-four is that if we put away our wickedness, our inclination towards this behavior, the prosperity of His presence will come our way. If we fill our minds and hearts up with His Word, verse twenty-two says He will deliver us and we will be at peace with Him.

It is impossible to be at peace with God and have sin in your life. Therefore, we must first accept Jesus, transfer from darkness into light, and we will be a peacemaker with God. Messed up since you've transferred? Confess, repent and be a peacemaker.

Secondly, some of us need to take our past life and make peace with it. Some of us have been raped, beaten, molested, verbally abused and deep down inside we harbor very bitter feelings. Notice verse fifteen of the twelfth chapter of Hebrews: "See to it that no one falls short of the grace of God and that no root of bitterness springs up, causing trouble and by it, defiling many." Bitterness is a killer. It is the natural response to our abuse and being harmed, but if left un-dealt with, it may kill you. It will not only physically kill you; it will also spiritually kill your church. You are not an island. Everything you've hidden in your soul will eventually leak out. When that happens, you will strike out at someone, probably an innocent someone, and the results are usually disastrous. Be a peacemaker.

The only power in the universe to aid you in removing bitterness is the power of God. Only God can hold your hand while you look and remember all that stuff that was done to you and only God can give you the power to let it all go. Be free from its slavery and make peace with who you are or what you were in the past.

> John 8:36 [36] Therefore if the Son [meaning Jesus] makes you free, you shall be free indeed. *NKJV* [6]

Finally, the passage above from Hebrews tells us to make peace with each other, especially our fellow children of light. Moreover, the apostle Paul wrote to the church in Rome:

> Romans 14:19 [19] So then, we must pursue what promotes peace and what builds up one another. *HCSB* [2]

What threatens the witness of most churches is what has threatened us for many, many years. Us. The people who call themselves "light" do more to stain the name of Jesus than any other agent by constantly fighting and arguing among ourselves. And, if I read the letters Paul wrote to the church at Corinth correctly, such behavior has only been going on for 2000 years. I and this piece of literature may exist for no other reason than to warn you about my home church and how NOT to behave.

When I was a child back in the early 1960's, my home church would run close to 200 people in Sunday School. More than once, I remember my dad and the other ushers coming up the stairs with folding chairs so that everyone could have a seat for the worship service. Times were good. Lives were being changed for the better and for all eternity. Then it happened.

Because of the phenomenal growth, it was obvious the church had to physically expand. However, there was a group of folks who really didn't like the pastor all that well and couldn't wait to get away. So it began. They fought over whether to build on the current site, or go somewhere else in town. They fought over expanding the current church, or to start a mission across town. After it was decided they would start a mission across town as well as remodel the current facility, they argued over who to hire for an architect. They fought over the color of the carpet, stained glass or no stained glass, and they fought and they fought and they fought. They fought over one silly thing or another for over twenty-five years. Twenty-five years, five pastors, eight new deacons later and they still fought. The church had three parking lots. At one point, things were so bad that the groups fighting each other would not even share the same parking lot. Childish, but true.

With every fight, every knock-down drag-out business meeting, a few folks would leave. Just a trickle at first. But then the exodus became more and more pronounced. More fighting, more folks leaving. The last time my family and I stepped foot into that church, the church I grew up in, the church where I met my wife, the church where my wife and I were married, attendance had gone from nearly 200 to 14. Our family of four was included in that number.

For twenty-five years, no one laid his or her agenda aside. Selfishness and childishness triumphed over peace and love while a dark world looked on from the outside. For twenty-five years, no one bothered to praise or build up his brother. No one bothered to be a peacemaker on any side. I understand that the doors of my home church are still open, but all the old members are gone and forgotten.

Be a peacemaker between you and God, be a peacemaker between yourself and your past, be a peacemaker among the children of light you worship with. Blessed are the peacemakers, they will be called the sons of God. If you are not sure that you and God have made peace, that you have passed from darkness to light, please see the end of the book for help.

Finally, here is one last truth. After you've made peace with God, He fights your remaining battles for you. The Deceiver of this world is not able to stand against Him who is called "The lion of the tribe of Judah." Victory in life is yours for the asking, but you first must be a peacemaker with God.

CHAPTER 7

A Father of Knowledge

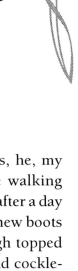

When my father was in his early teens, he, my uncle Leonard and Granddad were walking through the woods going back home after a day in town. As they walked, Granddad admired the new boots that he had just purchased. They were shiny, high topped boots that would protect his legs from thorns and cockle-burs. Suddenly, Dad and Leonard gasped. In front of them, crossing their path, was the largest snake they had seen in some time. I apologize to you that I can not recall the breed of snake that it was, but it was nonpoisonous and huge. At that moment, Dad said a strange fire appeared in Granddad's eyes.

"Boys, I'm going to show you one way to kill a snake."

With that, Granddad took off running towards the snake. About two-thirds of the way to where the snake lay, Granddad jumped into the air, much as a long jumper would hurl himself toward the landing pit. As he flew through the air, Granddad crouched into position to land, with his toes pointed skyward and the heels of his new boots pointed down. My Dad understood that it was Granddad's intention to land on the snake's head heels first, the force of the blow killing the reptile and ending the battle with one strike. There was only one problem. No one consulted the snake.

As Granddad was air borne, the snake coiled up and prepared for the upcoming fight. Sure enough, instead of Granddad landing on the snake's head, he landed in the middle of a battle ready beast. Dad said you never saw such screaming, kicking and jumping in all your life as the man desperately tried to get out of the mess he now found himself in. Granddad made moves that Dad and Uncle Leonard had never witnessed any human ever making. He kicked higher than a Radio City Music Hall Rockette.

After a pitched battle that lasted a few minutes, the snake slithered off into the brush, completely unharmed and none the worse for the wear. And there stood Granddad, embarrassed and humiliated in front of two teen-aged boys who were desperately holding their laughter. After a few moments, Granddad, always a man of few words, spoke again.

"Well boys, let this be a lesson to ya'. Sometimes things don't turn out the way you've got 'em planned."

Of all the words Granddad spoke, perhaps these are the most filled with wisdom. Sometimes, things don't resolve themselves in a way we could foresee or plan for. Life sometimes alters its course without consulting us in advance. I'm sure September 11, 2001 will always stick with me as a day my life was changed. As I watched the events of that day unfold on television, I knew that life from that point on would be much different. Perhaps your life was changed even more than mine. How then, do you set goals and make plans for the future when the bedrock of life appears to be more like shifting sand?

First of all, don't depend on yourself alone. The wisdom of the Proverbs tells us:

> Proverbs 14:12 There is a way *that seems* right to a man, But its end *is* the way of death. *NKJV* [6]

and

> Proverbs 12:15 The way of a fool seems right to him, but a wise man listens to advice. *NIV* [4]

Both of these verses speak of the dangers of going it alone. As romantic as the world fabricates it to appear, the Bible calls setting our own course and living life our way foolish and a path to certain death. Remember, God is light. Light is a giver of life. Men love darkness rather than light and the result of darkness is eternal death. Going it alone through life is deadly. This begs the questions, "Whom then should we listen to for advice?" and "Whom should we invite to go through life with us?"

Well, let's see. Perhaps we should trust people who have their pulse on the future. After all, there are many intelligent people who are trained to comprehend what the future holds and to chart a safe path. I could trust my stockbroker or my banker. But every time I call on these guys, they tell me how there are no guarantees. Similarly, my lawyer can help me make plans, but he can not guarantee those plans are fail safe. I usually call my physician only after I'm sick. He never calls me with an advanced warning.

"Hello?"

"Paul, this is Dr. Smith. In 48 hours you will have a high fever and chills symptomatic of the flu. I suggest you start forcing liquids now and get plenty of rest."

That has never happened to me. If those fortunetellers on TV can see so far in the future, why can't they predict when the police will show up and raid their files? Whom can I depend upon to know my tomorrows?

> Psalm 139:16 [16]You saw me before I was born. Every day of my life was recorded in your book. Every moment was laid out before a single day had passed. NLT [3]

Here is an amazing fact. God saw you before you were born and understood every decision each day of your life would hold, the consequences of each alternative to that decision, the joy of choosing right and the pain of choosing wrong. He understood all that and recorded it as HISTORY BEFORE you were born. Therefore, sometimes things don't work out the way we have them planned, but they always go according to God's knowledge because He sees the end from the beginning. Who better to go to for advice about your decisions than God?

Asking God for advice is not some kind of magic potion. God is not in the fortune telling business. He is, however, able to pass along tidbits of His knowledge to those who walk with Him by faith. Consider the following from the Gospel of John:

> John 12:35–36a [35]Jesus answered, "The light will be with you only a little longer. Walk while you have the light, so that darkness doesn't overtake you. The one who walks in darkness doesn't know where he's going. [36]While you have the light, believe in the light, so that you may become sons of light." HCSB [2]

Jesus said that throughout our lives, occasionally each of us will receive a glimpse of His light. For some, the only time we see that light is when we sense an overwhelming need to pass from darkness into light. If we reject that impression, we may never experience His light in our lives again. Jesus said those who do reject the need for Him walk in darkness and don't know where they are going. Do you want a true barometer of your spiritual life? If you are unsure of your eternal destination, either with God or away from God, you are in darkness because you don't know where you are going. Christians, the people of light, know they are going to be with God. The apostle John tells us again:

> 1 John 5:12–13 [12]The one who has the Son [Jesus] has life. The one who doesn't have the Son of God does not have life. [13]I have written these things to you who believe in the name of the Son of God, so that you may know that you have eternal life. HCSB [2]

If you take part in no religious activity whatsoever or you walk with Jesus but you are unsure of your eternal destiny, you are walking in darkness and I urge you to turn to the light. If you are a very religious person, but your faith teaches that you cannot know for sure that you are bound for heaven, I urge you to turn to the True Light. John teaches us that we can KNOW about tomorrow because our lives are held by the One who sees tomorrow as history. For more information on turning from darkness to light, see the end of the book.

Jesus said that if you believe in Him, you will "become the sons of light." Since God is light and we are becoming the sons of light, this implies that every Christian has the privilege of asking the living God for advice about any matter that concerns us. By faith, if we listen to the moving of Holy Spirit, our decisions will be based on His knowledge. As I've said before, this is not magic, it's faith. It does NOT mean we will always choose the right stock, predict the weather better than the National Weather Service or always pick the quickest line in the grocery store. It does mean that our lives will be changed to fit His will. If we selfishly think that, if God (who knows the right stock to choose, the weather forecast and the quickest line in the grocery store) can give us glimpses of His light and thus make us wealthy, we fail to appreciate that we've just turned God Almighty into an idol for our benefit. It is faith and not magic, because every glimpse of His light will for eternity change and mold me into a likeness that pleases Him, not the other way around. He knows the end from the beginning and knows the attributes I need to get through tomorrow. Thus I am wise to let Him mold me into what He knows I need to be to obtain victory over the pains and temptations of tomorrow. Whom should you turn to for plans and advice about the future? GOD!

No wonder the writer of the book of wisdom known as Proverbs wrote:

> Proverbs 3:5–6 ⁵Trust in the LORD with all your heart, And lean not on your own understanding; ⁶In all your ways acknowledge Him, And He shall direct [make smooth and straight] your paths. *NKJV* ⁶

And the prophet Jeremiah wrote:

> Jeremiah 29:11 ¹¹"For I know the plans I have for you," says the LORD. "They are plans for good and not for disaster, to give you a future and a hope." *NLT* ³

While the events of Tuesday, September 11, 2001 may have altered our plans and lives, know that the plan God has for us did not change. The events of that day should not have us asking "Where was God?", but rather those events clearly show us how far a deceived people will go in scattering their darkness. God is where He has always been, on His throne. Disaster and death happen because some people choose to walk in darkness rather than light. Those who performed those acts will eternally bear the shame of their actions.

As my Granddad turned to face his sons, he was embarrassed and ashamed to admit he was unable to extinguish a snake. His plan was not perfect. The plans you construct on your own will not be perfect. But if we acknowledge God in every detail of our lives, even when things appear to be terrible, He is still able to make our way smooth and straight.

First point: We should not base our plans on our own perceptions, but seek the counsel of God. Second point: The counsel of God is found in His Word, the Holy Bible.

Consider closely the words of the psalmist and the apostle Peter:

Psalm 119:105 [105]Your word *is* a lamp to my feet And a light to my path. *NKJV* [6]

and

2 Peter 1:19 [19]So we have the prophetic word strongly confirmed. You will do well to pay attention to it, as to a lamp shining in a dismal place, until the day dawns and the morning star [Jesus] arises in your hearts. *HCSB* [2]

Since God is light, His Word, the Bible, should also be a part of that light. Careful study of the Word of God implants that light into us. The correct use of the light derived from God is what wisdom is all about. The plans made for your life and mine should be based on the advice of God. That advice is derived from the study of God's Word. Wisdom is the correct application of the Word to our plans and lives.

Notice that the apostle Peter advises us to pay attention to God's Word. He says it shines as a light in a dismal place. Are you hopeless? You *are* in a dismal place. Are you uncertain about what tomorrow holds? You *are* in a dismal place. Is there no sense of direction for your life? You *are* in a dismal place. Unfortunately, I too have visited many of these same dismal places. How did I find my way out? By paying attention to God's Word. If God sees the end from the beginning, then He can cause a man thousands of years ago to write words to help me today. Scientists report that physical light travels through time and space at a speed of 186,000 miles per second. Spiritual light can also travel at astonishing speed. God's aid and advice can transcend time to meet your need today if you pay attention to what the Word says.

The plans we make in our own power always fall short of our expectations. Plans made based on the Word of God never disappoint.

CHAPTER 8

The Milk Cow Blues and a Father Who Provides

Whatcha doin', Paul?" my Aunt Dorothy asked my dad.

"I'm fixin' to go for a ride. Wanna come along?"

"Well, I guess. Kinda boring though, just you pullin' me around in your wagon."

"I'm not goin' to be pullin' nothin'."

"Well, if you ain't gonna be pullin', how are you takin' me for a ride?"

"Bessie'll do the pullin'."

"Bessie! Bessie cain't pull anything! She's a cow!"

"Shhhh! Mom's gonna hear you! Now hush while I try and go catch her."

Thus the conversation went the day my dad decided to play cowboy. Being a boy aged nine years or so, the American cowboy had a great appeal for my dad. Lindbergh had yet to make his great journey across the Atlantic, so the cowboy was the great American icon. Having a real live gun-carrying lawman in the family (George McQueen of chapter six) didn't help much, either. Cowboy fever had my dad in its grasp and wasn't about to let go. So, my dad was inspired to author the following plan based on the great migration west by pioneers in wagons:

a) Use little red wagon obtained at Christmas as a replacement for Springfield horse drawn wagon.
b) Obtain horse. Since horse is not available, use Bessie the milk cow as replacement.
c) Tie Bessie to wagon using rope number one.
d) For steering, tie rope number two to Bessie's halter.
e) To get Bessie to pull, use buggy whip found in barn.

The plan appeared fail safe. Since at age nine you don't have a great eye for detail, it escaped him that he hadn't considered a way to get Bessie to stop when needed. The word "Whoa" means a great deal to a well-trained horse, but to a stressed out milk cow on the run, it would prove to mean very little.

Bessie had been on the farm for a time and was a gentle beast of the Jersey breed. Easily caught and easily lead, it didn't take much effort for Dad to catch her and lead her to the wagon. She stood remarkably still as Dad tied a rope to both sides of her halter and then tossed the end of the rope over her back and on to the wagon. Furthermore, she stood still as Dad tied the main rope to the end of the wagon handle in a hard knot. After all, you don't want your "horse" getting away from you on the trail. If a hard knot was good to secure the wagon, then surely a hard knot was okay for Bessie's tail. Thus, he tied the other end of the rope to Bessie's tail in a hard knot.

"You ready to go, Sissy?" Dad asked Dorothy.

"I guess," was her weak reply as she climbed into the wagon behind Dad.

Dad grabbed the whip, popped it over Bessie's head and screamed "Heeya!"

Scared out of her wits, Bessie leaped forward only to feel a terrible pain shoot through her tail. This, of course, led her to jump again, but this time with more velocity and muscle. The pain struck her again in the tail, but this time it was worse as the hard knot Dad had tied clenched down even tighter. This produced another leap and a gallop and Bessie was at full speed headed out the driveway. After the rough start, Dad had dropped the rope that was to be his steering mechanism and now he and Dorothy were at the mercy of Bessie the run-away cow. Without knowing it, Dad had invented the first, nearly perfect, perpetual motion machine by tying that hard knot onto Bessie's tail. The more she jumped and ran, the more it hurt so the more she would jump and run.

Grandma Bond stood and looked out her kitchen window to see if she could tell what the commotion was all about. Who knows what went through her mind when one milk cow (eyes bugged out and full of fear), two white-faced kids (her darling little babies obviously in great dread of what the next few moments had in store) and one little red wagon went flying by the window. All she could think of to do was to scream and run out of the house in pursuit of those she cared for. This was and wasn't a good thing, for every time Grandma yelled, Bessie would run still faster, trying to make her escape from the pain which had engulfed her tail. On the other hand, Grandma was able to observe the outcome of this ordeal and to check on the well being of her babies in the run-away red wagon.

As they approached the end of the drive, Dad let go of the buggy whip and grabbed on to the sides of the wagon. "Hold on!" he yelled back at Dorothy. Somehow, I don't believe at this point Dorothy needed much encouragement to hold on to something. At the end of the drive, Bessie turned right and headed south down what is now known as Razorback Road. The wagon bounced, but didn't turn over, as Dad and Dorothy leaned into the turn. Quickly, the lane turned from peaceful byway on Fayetteville's west side into the Bond family circus: Bessie (the half mad cow), Paul and Dorothy (young children in desperate need of rescue) and giving chase in hot pursuit, Grandma.

While it was a little late at this point to consider a braking system, as the spectacle continued down the road, Dad was able to get a few "Whoa, Bessie!" shouts to leave his mouth. As mentioned earlier, they had little effect on the poor bovine who by now was convinced the pain shooting up her tail and backbone might not ever end. Those along the road who witnessed this "parade" would either stop and just stare, or they gave only a half-hearted attempt at stopping the cow.

Running at full speed, it didn't take Bessie long until she ran a half mile south and approached another corner. This time, however, the dirt lane would give way, not to another dirt lane, but to the newly paved U.S. Highway 62 and all its traffic. Once again, Dad yelled out to his fellow passenger, "Hang on!" as Bessie rounded the corner and headed east towards town.

"My babies!" Grandma yelled in horror as the wagon once again skipped and bounced around the corner. Exhausted from all her running, she stopped and did all she could think of to do: she prayed.

With wagon full of kids in tow, Bessie the runaway milk cow was now Bessie the missile. Running down U.S. 62, Bessie was able to convince every vehicle she met that she meant business as she forced car after car off the road. Horns blared out a non-ending chorus of "Ah-OOO-ga's" and tires squealed as vehicles turned in any direction possible to avoid the half mad cow.

Through all the noise and commotion, Grandma kept praying.

Finally, there was one man driving a Model-T Ford who saw the situation and had an idea about what to do. Just at the place where the Frisco Railroad overpass crossed over the highway, this man pulled his car sideways across the two lane road and stopped.

The great thing about cows is the fact that they are not horses. When a horse is scared, it can run full gallop for two to three miles. Cows, on the other hand, tend to tire out after a mile or three quarters of a mile. As Bessie approached the Frisco overpass, she was about to hit the one mile mark. Seeing the automobile across the road, Bessie slowed down to look for an alternate route. As she slowed, Bessie must have noticed the pain in her tail decreased slightly. Would slowing down more stop the pain completely? As Bessie slowed to a halt, the man in the Model-T jumped out of his car and grabbed Bessie's halter.

"They're saved!" Grandma heard someone exclaim. Her eyes opened from the prayer she had been voicing. Quickly, she jumped on the running board on a car driven by someone headed toward the scene. As she arrived, she found her children alive and well. Dorothy was crying. Dad was wide-eyed and un-talkative. But both children were safe. Bessie the cow was panting severely, but unhurt. It all could have been much worse. But God is a Father who provides. He provides more for us than any of us will ever truly understand. There are four things that the Bible speaks of God providing. These are safety, shelter, salvation and hope for tomorrow.

Since God is light, surely there is safety in being in the presence of that light. Danger usually dwells in darkness. Light provides protection. That God provides safety is a concept based primarily in the Old Testament. In the book of Proverbs we read:

> Proverbs 29:25 [25]Fear of man will prove to be a snare,
> but whoever trusts in the LORD is kept safe. *NIV* [4]

Other Scriptures that reinforce this concept that God provides safety to those who trust Him are found in Leviticus 25:18–19, Psalm 4:8 and Proverbs 18:10. However, we also know that there is an entire book of the Bible, the book of Job, that tells of a man who believed in and obeyed God, and yet he suffered numerous heartaches and disasters. What does it mean then, when the Bible says, "but whoever trusts in the Lord is kept safe?"

Let's consider Job for a moment. Many of us have heard of Job, but not many of us truly understand what he went through, what he lost and what he kept. The first chapter of Job clearly tells us that what happened to him was a test. In order to test his spiritual fortitude, God allowed several terrible things to happen in Job's life. God may also test your faith and spiritual fortitude one day. Perhaps you are being tested even now. I heard someone say that you should always remember that, like a wise schoolteacher, God never gives you a test unless He is sure you've prepared for the examination. Job was prepared for his exam because he never blamed God for all that he lost.

What Job lost was all ten of his children and all his livestock. In the early days of the Old Testament, a man's wealth was measured in how many livestock he owned. Thus, in a way, Job lost all his wealth as well. In terms of dollars, what Job lost was in excess of $10 million. But I am sure two things broke his heart more than money: burying ten children and having the love of his life, his wife, advising him to "curse God and die." But in spite of all he lost, we never remember what Job retained. He kept his faith and his relationship with the living God.

Perhaps then, what the word "safety" means is not necessarily physical safety, but spiritual safety. In the incident above, the life of my father and aunt were spared due to the prayers of my grandmother. Thus, there are times when trusting in God does result in physical safety for the ones we love as well as ourselves. This probably occurs more often than we realize; it's just that in this scientific and technical world we live in, we usually give credit for our safety to other things. However, being spiritually safe is far more important. What good is there in trusting a god who can't or won't guarantee the security and deliverance of your soul? Very little. The good news is that, the Living God, the Light, is the only God who promises us spiritual safety. In Isaiah we read:

> Isaiah 43:13b [13]". . . No one can deliver out of my hand. When I act, who can reverse it?" NIV [4]

and from the Gospel of John:

> John 10:28–30 [28]"I [Jesus] give them eternal life, and they will never perish—ever! No one will snatch them out of My hand. [29]My father, who has given them to Me, is greater than all. No one is able to snatch them out of the Father's hand. [30]The Father and I are one." HCSB [2]

Thus, with God, we can be assured that our most important possession, our life to come, is kept safe in His hand. Yes, there can be physical safety in trusting God, but there is ALWAYS spiritual safety in knowing and trusting

God. When God acts, nothing can reverse that activity. If I am in the hand of God, nothing can pull me out or steal me away. If your salvation depends upon Him, it sounds like you're in good shape. If your salvation depends upon some good works you feel you need to do, you may want to consider fire insurance. If you're not sure where to obtain fire insurance, see the end of the book for help.

God is also a provider of our daily physical needs such as shelter. Consider the words from the Gospel of Matthew:

> Matthew 6:31–33 [31]So don't worry, saying, 'What will we eat?' or 'What will we drink?' or 'What will we wear?' [32]For the Gentiles [literally non-Jewish people; figuratively, the people who walk in darkness] eagerly seek all these things, and your heavenly Father knows that you need them. [33]But seek first the kingdom of God and His righteousness, and all these things will be provided for you. HCSB [2]

Our heavenly Father knows you need the basic provisions of life. He provided these things to every patriarch of the Old Testament. When Abraham left Ur with his flocks and herds and moved to Haran and then to the Promised Land, every night God provided pasture and water for Abraham's livestock, food for his servants and a place to pitch his tent. When Moses led the Israelites out of Egypt, God provided bread from heaven called manna, quail for meat and water from the rocks. When Elijah ran from King Ahab, he camped by a stream and ravens brought him morsels of food. God always provided for the sons of His own family. God can and will provide for you. It is a matter of faith to believe God will do what He says he will do.

But notice that there is an attitude thing that goes along with this. First of all, our daily needs should not be the center of our universe, the object of our worry nor the energy that motivates us to action. In verse thirty-two above, Jesus said that those who walk in darkness are preoccupied with obtaining stuff to use and to satisfy their own appetites. Has anyone heard of a consumer-driven society? A person who is driven by materialism will always say the following phrases:

"I've got to get one of those."

"It sure would be nice to have one of them."

"Well, I know what my spouse just bought me for Christmas!"

People who are driven by consuming things are empty people because they use and devour what makes them happy. What happens when they don't have things to consume? They worry. What happens when they don't have money to buy the things to consume? Worry. What good does worry accomplish? None. Can I get myself to the moon by worrying? Can I control the stock market by worrying? Can I change jobs by worrying? No, no and no. If you feel empty and are worried, here's God prescription for relief: pursue the things of God first, and then God will provide your basic needs. Basic needs do NOT include cell phones, DVD players, televisions, VCR's, microwave ovens, computers, palm pilots, scanners, digital cameras . . . well, you get the picture. Realize that everything you have has come to you through the blessing of God. Ask Him how you are to use what you've been given for His glory. If His work and glory needs to be expanded through you, you will receive what you need to carry out the job.

God is the provider of salvation. In recent years, several imitators have appeared on the scene. Those who are absorbed by New Age thought will tell you that these other providers of a way to heaven are just as good as, if not equal to, the God of the Bible. Their argument sounds very convincing. Getting to heaven is just like getting to the old Union Station in St. Louis. Several tracks owned by several different railroads run to the same station. But instead of Missouri Pacific, Rock Island, or Frisco, these railroads are called Islam, Buddhism or the Church of Latter-Day Saints. It really doesn't matter which of these you take, because you reach the same place, so they tell you. Since New Age thinkers see everything as being one, it is irrelevant what you believe or how fervently you believe since we all are part of the divine. Unfortunately for them, the Bible rejects this notion. Consider:

> Isaiah 43:11 [11]I, *even* I, *am* the LORD, and besides Me *there is* no savior. NKJV[6]

and

> John 14:6 [6]Jesus told him, "I am the way, the truth, and the life. No one comes to the Father except through Me. HCSB [2]

Both God the Father, in the Old Testament, and Jesus in the New Testament, tell us the same thing: there are not multiple ways to heaven, but only one. God alone has provided salvation, none other need apply. None other has been so equipped. None other is a god of love like Jehovah God, the living God and the Light. All these are names of the same railroad track to that one destination we all long to see.

Serving the living God gives you hope for tomorrow. I will trouble you to read one more Scripture. The prophet Jeremiah witnessed the fall of Jerusalem in 586 B.C., the burning of the holy temple and the utter destruction of the city at the hands of the Babylonian army. All he ever knew or loved was destroyed and lay smoldering. The beauty of the City of David was all gone. All that was left was rubble. However, he took pen in hand and wrote:

Lamentations 3:19–23 [19]I remember my affliction and my wandering, the bitterness and the gall. [20]I well remember them, and my soul is downcast within me. [21]Yet this I call to mind and therefore I have hope: [22]Because of the LORD's great love we are not consumed, for his compassions never fail. [23]They are new every morning; great is your faithfulness. *NIV* [4]

After the recent events in our country, many of us appear to be discouraged or lack hope. Where there is light, there is always hope. God is light.

Before the day my dad decided to play cowboy, I am not sure he understood the power of prayer. I am uncertain whether Grandma Bond, in the whole rest of her life, ever prayed a prayer that was as effective as the one petition she offered to God that day. But after it was all over, and perhaps some time had passed, I think the three of them understood that there is a God who provides just when we need Him to. I don't think that the man in the Model-T was known by my grandmother or whether she ever saw him again. But that day, because of prayer, he was used as an instrument of God. Have you ever experienced the power of the living God working through you? If not, you may want to read the end of the book on how we can pass from darkness to light.

CHAPTER 9

Hawk and Cynthy and a Father Who Waits

My mom turned over in bed and tried to bring the alarm clock into focus. "What time is it?" she wondered. She grabbed the clock and turned it to catch a small beam of light coming through the bedroom window. "Two o'clock in the morning. Yup. That's what it says; 2 A.M."

As she sat the clock back down on the dresser, she caught a glimpse of something moving out on the lawn. She sat up to investigate.

Outside the wind was blowing, lightening flashed and thunder rumbled as a thunderstorm approached from the northwest. Peering out the window, Mom saw a female figure dressed in white walking back and forth on the lawn. Occasionally the figure would stop and turn northward as if looking towards the end of the street.

"Is this a ghost?" Mom wondered. "Or just a mirage?" Squinting through the darkness to try and get a closer look, Mom found the truth. It was neither a ghost nor a mirage. It was Cynthy walking around the yard in her white flannel nightgown and a white scarf waiting once again for Hawk to come home. She would look earnestly toward the end of the street to look for the headlights of Hawk's truck. On this night, as on many other nights, Hawk would not be turning the corner to come home. Cynthy, however, kept her vigil.

At his birth, he was named George Washington Bond. Everyone who knew him just called him Hawk. In Arkansas, we have a strange custom. What you look like, how you appear to others, is what your nickname becomes. Hawk had the trademark large nose of the Bond clan and always kept a flat-top haircut. Thus, to look at him, it was obvious why he was called Hawk. He looked like a hawk. If God wills that I should pen another book, I may tell you about Donkey Smith or Frog Chambers.

Hawk was a stonemason by trade, but here in the waning days of the Great Depression, demand for stonemasons was poor as few houses were being built. Thus, Hawk and his wife Cynthy lived in the basement of my grandfather's house until they could get back on their feet. Likewise, my mom and dad, being newlyweds, were living with Grandma and Granddad Bond until they could get a start in life. Mom would always remember this spring night of 1938 as the night she saw her first "ghost."

As you might have guessed by now, besides being a stonemason, Hawk was also a ne'er-do-well and a dreamer who never earned a great deal of money or the respect of his brothers. In short, Hawk was the black sheep of his family. This in turn brought on occasional bouts of drinking and getting drunk. On this particular night, as Cynthy paced the lawn before the storm started, waiting for him to come home, Hawk was drying out in the Washington County Jail.

The family looked down on Hawk not only because he was prone to drink and a ne'er-do-well, but also because he married Cynthy. You see, Cynthy was at least three-quarters, if not full blooded Cherokee and this was her second marriage. In the twenty-first century it is hard to imagine the stigma surrounding being married to a divorcee. Moreover, this was a mixed race marriage, which wasn't acceptable to some members of the community either. At sunrise, after the storm, Cynthy walked the three miles to the jailhouse. Sure enough, her husband was a prisoner. Hawk could not come home right away, she found out, as his truck veered off the road and struck the side of a gas station. The sheriff was waiting to see if the owner was going to press charges other than drunk driving. Unable to raise bail, Cynthy did what you would expect of her once you came to know her. She went outside, sat down on the jailhouse steps, and waited for Hawk to be released. She waited day and night, day after day, until Hawk had served his time.

Cynthy's actions embarrassed some members of the family no end. You see, the main highway through Northwest Arkansas, U.S. 71, ran right in front of the jailhouse in those days. Anyone coming into town, stranger or local, would notice the skinny little Indian woman sitting on the jailhouse steps. It's bad enough she's an Indian and a divorcee, but does she have to sit there like that? While the family was afraid of ridicule, it was mostly Cynthy that bore the brunt of the shame. No matter. She would wait on the man she loved. When Hawk was finally released, she reacted as only Cynthy could. She shook her head and muttered, "You've been a naughty boy" and walked her husband home.

So what's this story all about? Three things.

First of all, just as Cynthy sat and waited patiently for her husband's release from jail, God patiently waits for you to decide that you want to be released from your bondage. In the book of Isaiah, we read these words:

> Isaiah 49:9 Through you [meaning Jesus] I am saying to the prisoners of darkness, "Come out! I am giving you your freedom!" *NLT*[3]

All of us have a choice. We can either choose to remain in the darkness of our prison cell that is referred to as "sin", or we can walk out. The thing that amazes me about the human race is how many people remain in their prison cell of mistakes, hard feelings and self pride rather than, by faith, walk out into the light of God. Who in their right mind would choose a prison cell over light and being free? Yet it happens every day. God still patiently waits for us to come to our senses. The apostle Paul wrote:

> 1 Timothy 1:16 [16]But I received mercy because of this, so that in me, the worst of them [sinners], Christ Jesus might demonstrate the utmost patience as an example to those who would believe in Him for eternal life. *HCSB*[2]

Do you understand what the apostle is saying? Here was an educated man, on his way upward through the levels of the religious aristocracy. He was so passionate about what he believed that he killed those who disagreed with his point of view. Yet, after he met Jesus Christ, he walked out of his prison of rules and regulations and became the greatest missionary of all time. Why? He said it was to demonstrate God's patience. At first this appears to be a self-abasing remark. In some ways it is. But what Paul's statement also implies is that God is so patient that He chooses to use mankind to introduce Himself to men. In this way, the power of God is seen through the one who delivers God's message as well as the hearer. God patiently waited for Paul to come to a place in his life where Paul was willing to change. In an instant, the light of God surrounded Paul and his life was changed forever. You can experience the same change, but you have to be willing to walk out of your prison cell.

Second, Cynthy suffered humiliation waiting on her husband's release. All who passed by the jailhouse laughed at the skinny Cherokee Indian woman waiting for her man. Jesus went through vast amounts of humiliation to establish a relationship with you. The Son of the living God was stripped of His clothes, spat upon, beaten, laughed at and executed so that one day, when the Spirit of God beckons, you could walk out of your prison.

Finally, Cynthy could not afford the bail needed to get Hawk out of jail. In your case and mine, things are entirely different. Jesus paid the price for your redemption (your release) from bondage. Once again I quote the apostle Paul:

Titus 2:14 [14]He gave Himself for us to redeem us from all lawlessness and to cleanse for Himself a special people, eager to do good works. *HCSB*[2]

Jesus endured the humiliation of a public execution to pay the price of your bail. Remember from chapter two how we discussed that the only way one could be forgiven from messing up was the blood of an innocent? Jesus came into this world, fully man and yet fully divine, to be that innocent. The price of your bail was paid in full through Him. You are free to walk away from your jail cell. When will you accept Him into your life and experience the change Paul experienced? Now? Please don't put the decision off. There is no guarantee of tomorrow. For additional help, see the appendix.

From Darkness to Light

Making sure that you have passed from darkness to light is as important to you as knowing the day you were born. Every day, since you were old enough to understand, the sun appears to rise in the eastern sky and wipe out every trace of the darkness of the night that has passed. Being of the Light is just as simple to understand. If you have the Light of Jesus in your life, you are of the light. If you are uncertain or unsure of your relationship with Him, you are still in darkness. However, once you have this question settled between you and God, you can rest assured that He is able to keep you supplied in light.

To pass from darkness to light, you have to understand four simple things:

1. Mankind is predisposed to do what is wrong, to mess up, and to fail to meet God's standards for our lives. Proverbs 4:19 tells us, "But the way of the wicked is

like deep darkness; they do not know what makes them stumble." (NIV[4]). Notice what this verse tells us. Because mankind is in the dark, those who try and walk through the darkness don't know where they are going and they keep stumbling and messing up. Romans 3:23 explains the situation this way: "For all have sinned and fall short of the glory of God." (NIV[4]).

2. While we were in darkness, stumbling around and hurting ourselves, a great thing happened. Light pierced through the darkness. Psalm 112:4 says, "Even in darkness light dawns for the upright . . ." (NIV[4]). Romans 5:8 explains it this way: "But God demonstrates his own love for us in this: While we were still sinners, Christ died for us." (NIV[4]). The death and resurrection of Jesus paid the penalty of your sin, your messing up, forever. Colossians 1:13–14 tells us, "For he has rescued us from the dominion of darkness and brought us into the kingdom of the Son he loves, in whom we have redemption, the forgiveness of sins." (NIV[4]).

3. You now face a choice. You can choose to be rescued and be a part of light, or you can choose to continue walking and stumbling in the dark. If you choose to remain in darkness, don't blame God if you stumble and hurt yourself again. The last phrase of 1 Peter 2:9 indicates that God is calling to you to walk out of the darkness and into the light. John 3:16 explains it this way: "For God so loved the world that he gave his one and only Son, that who-

ever believes in him shall not perish but have eternal life." (NIV[4]). If you choose light, you must have God help you turn your life into a new direction. Romans 13:12 says "The night is nearly over; the day is almost here. So let us put aside the deeds of darkness and put on the armor of light." (NIV[4]).

4. Realize that since you have chosen light, and agreed to let God help you turn your life around, you are no longer the same person. Inside your heart, you are much different now. Ephesians 5:8–11 instructs you how you are to behave after this change in your life: "For you were once darkness, but now you are light in the Lord. Live as children of light (for the fruit of the light consists in all goodness, righteousness and truth) and find out what pleases the Lord. Have nothing to do with the fruitless deeds of darkness . . ." (NIV[4]).

If you understand all that you've read to this point, and you wish to choose light over darkness, say this prayer to God:

Dear Heavenly Father, I come to you as a part of the darkness, but I want to be a child of the Light. Thank You for Jesus, that He died on the cross in my place and for my sin. I ask now that you forgive me of my darkness. Come into my heart, be Lord of my life and I will forever follow after you. In Jesus' name, Amen.

If you said that prayer and meant it, you are now an adopted child of the Most High God. Begin to study His Word. You may wish to read first the book of 1 John or perhaps the Gospel of Luke. Find a church that proclaims God's word as truth and become committed to those fellow believers in Christ. I look forward to meeting you one day in heaven at the feet of Jesus.

References

1. The Index of Leading Cultural Indicators; ©1999, William J. Bennett, Broadway Books, publishers, 1540 Broadway, New York, NY 10036; page 48.
2. Unless otherwise noted, Scripture quotations marked HCSB have been taken from the Holman Christian Standard Bible, © Copyright 2000 by Holman Bible Publishers. Used by permission.
3. Unless otherwise noted, Scripture quotations marked NLT have been taken from the Holy Bible, New Living Translation, copyright ©1996 by Tyndale Charitable Trust. All rights reserved.
4. Scripture quotations marked NIV taken from the HOLY BIBLE, NEW INTERNATIONAL VERSION, Copyright 1973, 1978, 1984 by the International Bible Society. Used by permission of Zondervan Publishing House. All rights reserved.

5. Experiencing God, Knowing and Doing the Will of God; 1990, Henry T. Blackaby and Claude V. King; published by Lifeway Press, 127 9th Ave. North, Nashville, TN 37234. All rights reserved, page 42.

6. Scripture quotations marked NKJV taken from The Holy Bible, New King James Version, copyright ©1982 by Thomas Nelson, Inc. Used by permission. All rights reserved.

To order additional copies of

FROM
MY

Lessons from Real Life

Have your credit card ready and call:

1-877-421-READ (7323)

or please visit our web site at
www.pleasantword.com

Also available at: www.amazon.com

Printed in the United States
1332900001B/34-42